Blessing
a dear au
friend & sister
in Christ ___
♡ Judith

GOD'S NEAR

is not an ordinary book!

GOD'S NEAR contains words of joy and wisdom that will bring comfort and inner peace.

GOD'S NEAR is a spiritual treasure of easy-to-read, poetic prose messages that will ease the pain and confusion of living in our tension-filled world. Revel in the truths of Christianity spoken through the author, who strives to listen to the voice of Christ daily.

You can be assured the living Christ is present. He is attentive to the smallest detail of your life, and He desires to reveal Himself as the worker of everything for good to those who love Him. You can be intimately connected with Him, the Creator of our Universe.

GOD'S NEAR

By Judith Rolfs

Dedication:
To God who deserves all glory!
"You are worthy, our Lord and God,
to receive glory and honor and power,
for you created all things,
and by your will they were created
and have their being."
Revelation 4:11

ISBN 978-0-9799895-4-4

ENDORSEMENTS:

"Uplifting Christian daily inspiration for living with hope and joy in our chaotic world. Each spiritual message conveys rich and probing thoughts."
Joann McLuen, Director of Women's Ministry

"Sound theology expressing the complex relationship of the soul with God. These are in perfect accord with traditional biblical doctrine expressed in a creative, engaging format."
Thomas Cavenagh, Author of *Jesus on Thursday*

"It only takes a moment. In these brief devotions I found my own emotions and needs exposed and soothed. I loved that the format allows the reader to just soak it in and found myself agreeing and worshipping. Let Judith pour God's Word and worship over your wounds too and feel your burdens lifted as you realize anew that God IS near."
Delores Liesner, Speaker, Author of *Be the Miracle*

"*God's Near* is written with God's heart in mind. A God of relationship, not religion. A God who loves His children unconditionally and beyond measure."
Pastor Chuck Sweetman, Delavan WI

Dear Readers,

These brief meditations are from my heart for your heart. The words came to me when I was longing for a sincere and genuine way to think about God and speak to Him. Day after day, I pored over the Bible on my knees or prostrate on the floor experiencing a thrilling, personal connection with Jesus. New thoughts came as I meditated on familiar Scriptures. I also spent time walking in nature saying, "Show me your glory, Lord," and over and over He *did*!

May these thoughts stimulate your own passion for God and His truth, and may you sense His living Presence with you. I pray your heart connection to God will grow stronger than you ever dreamed possible.

Judith

Lord of Love

Lord of love,
I thought my life needed something more,
I crammed my world with things,
And stuffed my days with experiences.

How confusing life was,
How amazing and simple it has become,
Lord of love,
You alone bring fullness to my life.

Slowly I've learned,
Having You alone,
Lord of love,
I have everything.

God's Word for You
*"But I trust in your unfailing love; my heart rejoices in
your salvation. I will sing to the LORD, for he has been
good to me." Psalm 13:5-6*

Days

Days slide together into a seamless strand,
Like water droplets over a waterfall.
Days filled with definite mistakes,
Often useless, irrational uncertainty
And chaotic moments lacking completion,
I'd like to snatch back a few and yell "Do-over."

I yearn to guard my days more closely,
And savor each one's sweetness
Before tomorrow slips into place.
All my past days have gone to You Lord,
Awaiting eternal examination.
May all my days, past and present, bring You glory.

God's Word for You
"For you have delivered me from death and my feet from stumbling, that I may walk before God in the light of life." Psalm 56:13

Guidance

Guide me Lord,
Establish my goals.
Left alone I might make them too high,
Or in timidity make too few.
Lord, You know my capability
And appropriate level of responsibility.

Guide me by Your spirit, Lord.
Send me wise mentors in the flesh too, please,
If You don't mind,
For human inspiration and affirmation.
But I give You total control, Lord,
Life goes best when You lead.

God's Word for You
"In your unfailing love you will lead the people you have redeemed. In your strength you will guide them to your holy dwelling." Exodus 15:13

Eighteen Years

For eighteen years the woman stooped,
Bent completely forward, unable to look upward,
Lord, You said,
A demon of sickness had deformed her
But You would make her right.

Lord, lay your hands on me as well.
May I always look upward,
Not bent by emotions or circumstances,
But walking tall and strong,
Made straight by Your hand.

God's Word for You
"On a Sabbath Jesus was teaching in one of the synagogues, and a woman was there who had been crippled by a spirit for eighteen years. She could not straighten up at all. When Jesus saw her, he said to her, 'Woman, you are set free from your infirmity.' Then he put his hands on her, and immediately she straightened up and praised God." Luke 13:10-13

Heaven's First Morning

I'd like to twirl with You, Lord,
And dance through the clouds.
May I ride the morning star?
I'd love to climb into Elijah's chariot
And see a startled fish from the splitting red sea.
May I pet the mane of Your white Horse,
And sit among the children You let come close?
Heaven's first morning will be so grand!

God's Word for You
"O Lord, God of Israel, there is no God like you in heaven above or on earth below-you who keep your covenant of love with your servants who continue wholeheartedly in your way." Exodus 15:13

Conversation With God

"Beloved, never let it be said,
That it's unusual for Me to speak to you.
I will speak to anyone who will listen.
Why would I not converse with my beloved?
Do humans not speak to those they love
And delight in intimate conversation?"

"Watch, for I also speak through creation.
Read Scripture, for many of my precious words
Are already recorded for all to know,
Yet never forget I still speak one on one
To waiting, loving hearts daily.
Come, listen."

God's Word for You

"The LORD came and stood there, calling as at the other times, "Samuel! Samuel! " Then Samuel said, "Speak, for your servant is listening." 1 Samuel 3:10

Those Moments

Lord, I don't believe I've ever said,
What it means to me to know
That You're always with me,
Whatever happens and wherever I go.

Lord, those moments when I'm low
When sickness comes out of nowhere,
And fills me with fear,
I need you near.
You flood me with hope,
Until wholeness again begins to flow.

Lord, those moments when I'm so very low
When insecurity comes out of nowhere,
And fills me with doubt,
I need You near.
You flood me with confidence.
And joy again begins to flow.

Lord, I don't believe I've ever said,
What it means to me to know
That You're always with me,
Whatever happens and wherever I go.

God's Word for You
"Whom have I in heaven but you?
And earth has nothing I desire besides you.
My flesh and my heart may fail, but God is the
strength of my heart and my portion forever."
Psalm 73:25-26

The Word

Lord, I come straight to You through Scripture,
Your Word of truth holds power.
It's my lifestyle-changer,
Mountain-mover,
Difference-maker,
Wisdom- source,
Fountain of encouragement.
Daily I open my God Book,
Your Holy Words,
For my Bible blessings.
I absorb Your principles,
Receive Your counsel.
Lord, I treasure Your truth.

God's Word for You
"I meditate on your precepts and consider your ways. I delight in your decrees; I will not neglect your Word." Psalm 119:15-16

Night Thoughts

In the middle of the night
When we're all alone,
Nobody but us Lord,

I sense Your presence
And feel Your glow all around me
Of shield, favor, and fire:

Your shield to guard me.
Your favor to bless me.
Your fire to ignite me.

In loving You,
I'm completely fulfilled,
And totally, authentically me.

God's Word for You
"On my bed I remember You; I think of You through the watches of the night. Because You are my help, I sing in the shadow of Your wings." Psalm 63:6,7

Moving Temples

Some sit in pretty pews
Or on soft, upholstered chairs,
And cozy up to one other at church suppers
Or weekly prayer-gossip sessions.

Pastors send flyers to the community
Inviting people to visit
Elders fawn over newcomers several times.
Then slip back to their comfy few.

The message is universal.
Come into church, be a regular attendee
Fatten our egos with attendance numbers.
Tithe on penalty of hell, isn't church swell?

But God You're not confined by walls.
You're best proclaimed from mountaintops
And displayed by love and joy in daily lives.
You're not a building or a program.

You've made us moving temples
Our torches a life-giving message.
You've made us to be on display
With words of truth and deeds of love.

God's Word for You
"What agreement is there between the temple of God and idols? For we are the temple of the living God. As God has said: 'I will live with them and walk among them, and I will be their God, and they will be my people.'"
2 Corinthians 6:16

14

Glory of God

Lord!
How could you do such an outrageous thing?
Making men and women in Your divine image!
Intending and even claiming
That we, your human creation,
Are the actual, living glory of God!
Lord, that means me, too!
How amazing!

God's Word for You
"O Lord, God of Israel, there is no God like you in heaven above or on earth below-you who keep your covenant of love with your servants who continue wholeheartedly in your way." 1 Kings 8:23

Good Night

Good night, Father,
Good night, Jesus,
Good night, Holy spirit.
Sleep is near.
As I drift into my rest.
Be with me,
This night, every night,
Forever.

God's Word for You
"By day the LORD directs his love, at night his song is with me - a prayer to the God of my life." Psalm 42:8

15

Messenger

Lord, You are absolutely real and true,
How sad that too few know You.

Lord, make me a messenger with power
That others' ears may tingle with truth.

May my love speak louder than the words I speak,
And may I be fully empowered by your Spirit.

Give me Your authority and boldness.
Anoint me as I proclaim Your reality.

God's Word for You
"Then Haggai, the LORD's messenger, gave this message of the LORD to the people: 'I am with you,' declares the LORD." Haggai 1:13

Creation

Lord, your process of creation fascinates me.
When darkness covered a formless earth,
And you chose to make it bright,
How did You know in advance
Light would be good?

Was it always Your plan to separate day from night?
What did You expect when You called dry land forth
From the expanse of waters under the heavens?
I'm not surprised that when You collected water for
the seas,
You stopped to give Your approval.

I would have liked to be there
When birds, and fish were spoken into existence
And blessed with the ability to multiply,
When animals strutted forth fit and pleasant.
Before the creation of male and female made in
Your image!

The lushness of vegetation yielding seed.
How good You declared Your infinite variety-
And Your reminders of providential care,
A sun and moon to mark seasons, days and years.
How clever of You, Lord.

The Presence

Lord, the aura of Your presence
Had to be overwhelming.
I can imagine why John fell asleep
When you appeared to him.

How can human senses absorb
Your supernatural essence?
The very thought of You thrills me!
In Your physical presence I'd surely swoon.

Yet, Lord, I yearn for the moment
Of being overcome by Your glory,
When we're face to face.
Only eternity in Your presence will be enough.

Creator

Creator of Light,
Maker of the Earth and me,
Without Your design
There would be none of this majesty.
How admirable Lord.

It had to be exciting Lord,
When You stood back and looked.
You'd never created a world before!
How excellent a masterpiece.
The land and seas, and everything else You made for me.

But Lord I wonder,
Why give complete authority over everything
To human heads and hands?
Dangerous don't You think?
Would You do it all over again?

You'd probably say yes,
You approved all You made,
And Lord so do I!
I'm grateful for this world
And everything in it.

God's Word for You
*"For by Him all things were created: things in heaven
and on earth, visible and invisible, whether thrones or
powers or rulers or authorities; all things were created
by Him and for Him. He is before all things, and in Him
all things hold together." Colossians 1:16-17*

Names

How awesome to have one's name announced
Before birth by God.
What an honor for
Isaac,
Solomon,
Josiah,
And John the Baptist!

I'm content to have my name merely known by You,
Lord!
What joy to be adopted into
The kingly heritage of my Lord of Lords.
I eagerly await the day
When I hear my name spoken aloud by You.
Lord, may it please You to add
Good and faithful.

God's Word for You
*"Glory in His holy name; let the hearts of those who
seek the Lord rejoice." Psalm 105:3*

Isaac

God wanted you called Isaac – laughter,
Your elderly mother-to-be Sarah laughed
When told of your approaching birth.
God admonished her for lack of faith.

Laughter at the right time is a gift.
At the wrong time it can be a curse,
When laughing signifies doubting God,
As Sarah discovered.

What a reminder that belief always brings blessings
Sarah spoke your name over and over with delight
All the rest of her life -
Isaac – laughter.

How like God to turn her error into blessing
When finally, she trusted.
Lord, I laugh also because of my confidence in You,
With exuberant, glorious jubilation!

God's Word for You
*"Sarah became pregnant and bore a son to Abraham
in his old age, at the very time God had promised him.
Abraham gave the name Isaac (laughter) to the son
Sarah bore him. Sarah said, 'God has brought me
laughter, and everyone who hears about this will
laugh with me.'" Genesis 21:2, 3, 6*

Carrier

Man of Sorrows they called You, Lord,
When they wounded You for my wrongs,
Chastised You without cause
To attain my good.

Carrier of my iniquities, wounded by whip straps,
Silent before tormentors
So that I could sing forever.
You secured my healings and wholeness.

You, who had no sin,
Chose to carry all mine.
You did this for me,
Precious, Sin-carrier divine.

God's Word for You
*"He was despised and rejected by men, a man of
sorrows, and familiar with suffering. He was despised,
and we esteemed him not." Isaiah 53:3*

Mary

Many a time in my imagination I flee, Mary,
To that special, safe place at your side.
How wonderful to know,
I have a perfect mother always near,
Whose love never fails me.
I'm so grateful for your presence
Every moment of my life.
Many a night you wiped away my tears.
And said, "Look up, for Jesus is near.
He came to earth through my body,
And paid your sin price through His sacrifice,
Jesus awaits your presence
At the right hand of the Father,
And His Holy Spirit is near."

God's Word for You
"But the angel said to her, 'Do not be afraid, Mary, you have found favor with God. You will be with child and give birth to a son, and you are to give him the name Jesus. He will be great and will be called the Son of the Most High.'" Luke 1:30-32

Parents

Parents, seek wisdom above all.
Make thinking and reflection
Your common household tools.
As the Queen of Sheba visited Solomon
 To experience his wisdom -
Which she knew to be
 Far more important than his wealth,
Seek daily more of God's truth,
Kept sacred and preserved
In Scripture and tradition.
Remember a dry well cannot give water.
Parents, future generations will be trained
By the inflow and outflow of your mind,
So, apply your knowledge from God to every endeavor.
Learn, love, and laugh
And your family will flourish.

God's Word for You
"My mouth will speak words of wisdom; the utterance from my heart will give understanding. I will turn my ear to a proverb; with the harp I will expound my riddle: Why should I fear when evil days come?"
Psalm 49:3-5

Almugwood

Lord, Your Word intrigues me.
In it I read of things I've never heard of -
Red sandalwood brought from Ophir.
Almugwood, sweet-smelling tree,
Strong almugwood used to make supports for your temple,
Yet, also pliable enough to form harps and lyres for musicians.
Lord, all your creation never ceases to amaze me.
How many lifetimes would I have to live
To comprehend all You have made?
O the richness, the variety, the complexity and the simplicity
Of You, Your work, and Your world.

God's Word for You
"Hiram's ships brought gold from Ophir; and from there they brought great cargoes of almugwood and precious stones. The king used the almugwood to make supports for the temple of the LORD and for the royal palace, and to make harps and lyres for the musicians. So much almugwood has never been imported or seen since that day." 1 Kings 10:11-12

Demons

Lord, Your people often don't realize
That it's demonic forces that bring them low.
Why do we hear few warnings about them?
How surprising since demons still roam,
Broken only by the power You bestow.

Times were different, Lord,
When You walked the earth.
Most people knew demons were real then
And talked about them freely.
They understood demons' power to torture and destroy.

Lord, just as You equipped the seventy You sent
To fight their demonic battles,
You equip us with strength and ability.
You promise that no demon
Can in any way harm us.

Lord, may I use Your power wisely,
Freeing those ensnared in thought or deed,
Who've been captured by demonic wiles,
Back to hell harbingers of deceit and death,
The Lord's power prevails still.

God's Word for You
"The Spirit clearly says that in later times some will abandon the faith and follow deceiving spirits and things taught by demons. Such teachings come through hypocritical liars, whose consciences have been seared as with a hot iron." 1 Timothy 4:1-2

26

Salt

Lord, I don't want to be:
Weak salt,
Flat salt,
Tasteless salt,
Fit- for- garbage salt.

Instead I yearn to be
Strong salt,
Preserving salt,
Heaven-bound salt.
Lord, may I be super-salty for Thee.

God's Word for You
"You are the salt of the earth. But if the salt loses its saltiness, how can it be made salty again? It is no longer good for anything." Matthew 5:13

Glory In

Jesus gloried in the Holy Spirit.
What does that mean?
To glory in You, Holy Spirit?
I yearn to know.
Why? Because I want this.
May it be true of me.

Holy Spirit, move upon me,
Flow around me.
Breathe within me.
Let Your breath become my breath.
Let Your desires become my desire.
Let Your fire become my fire.

God's Word for You
"But you will receive power when the Holy Spirit comes on you; and you will be my witnesses in Jerusalem, and in all Judea and Samaria, and to the ends of the earth." Acts 1:8

Sheep Hunt

Lord, some dear people I know
Have lost their way.
Words aren't reaching them.
They refuse to hear what I say.

Lord, go after them please.
I'm on my knees.
These people are such a treasure.
I truly love them beyond measure.

I can't bear for them to be lost.
What a waste of their Kingdom potential!
But all my efforts have been as nothing.
If only they can be reached.

Lord, go after them please
Shepherd them to safety,
Use Your staff if You must,
Do whatever it takes to get them home.

God's Word for You
"The Lord says: I myself will search for my sheep and look after them." Ezekiel 34:11

Healing Faith

Faith for healing?
Having confidence in You, Lord.
That's all it takes?
Mere faith in Your supernatural power?
You've made healing this easy?
Only trust and believe You say.
And remember all will be healed someday,
Whether on earth or in heaven, and
A healthy soul takes priority over bodily health.
Lord such a simple plan.
Surely, I can accomplish this. Help me, I pray,
Be faith filled each day.
Your Scriptures are filled with healing stories.
Luke 17:19 "Then he said to him, 'Rise and go;
your faith has made you well.'"
Luke 7:50 "Jesus said to the woman,
'Your faith has saved you; go in peace.'"
Luke 8:47-48 "Then he said to her, 'Daughter,
your faith has healed you. Go in peace.'"
Mark 10:51-52 "The blind man said, 'Rabbi, I want to see.'
'Go,' said Jesus, 'Your faith has healed you.'
Immediately he received his sight
and followed Jesus along the road."
Lord, I believe. Help my unbelief.

"Truly I tell you, if you have faith as small as a mustard seed, you can say to this mountain, 'Move from here to there,' and it will move. Nothing will be impossible for you." Matthew 17:20

Everything

Selling all?
Surrendering lordship over possessions?
Changing priorities?
For endless possibilities with God?
Some may hesitate,
But not me, not for a second.
What an easy decision.
Lord, I choose the treasure of You.
Only make me worthy
To receive all You promise.

God's Word for You
"Jesus answered, 'If you want to be perfect, go, sell your possessions and give to the poor, and you will have treasure in heaven. Then come, follow me.'"
Matthew19:21

The Judge

Widow, you annoyed the judge
When you sought
Justice and protection.
You refused to be denied
And wouldn't stop badgering him.

You gave that unjust judge
Incredible annoyance,
Even fear he'd be assaulted or strangled.
He knew you'd persist
Until you were avenged.

Lord, You are my great and just judge,
You're always available
And forever willing to help me.
And my persistent asking pleases You.
So, Lord, I shall ask and ask.

God's Word for You
*"Blessed are all who fear the Lord, who walk in His
ways. You will eat the fruit of your labor; blessings
and prosperity will be yours. Thus is the man [or
woman] blessed who fears the Lord. May the Lord
bless you from Zion all the days of your life."*
Psalm 128: 1, 2, 4, 5

Mystery

The people walked next to Living Truth, Lord,
Yet comprehended You not.
The Word remained mystery,
You were flogged, killed, arose.

Their blind minds saddened You,
More than their jeers and spit.
Releasing their anguish and bondage
Was Your only wish.

Some came near to abandoning fear
Yet for many sad souls
 Truth remained unclaimed.
The Word remained mystery.

God's Word for You
*"But the eyes of the Lord are on those who fear him,
on those whose hope is in his unfailing love."*
Psalm 33:18

Lucky Colt

Lucky colt, untied for a King's ride,
Brought as bidden to Jesus.
For a ride that would lead to His betrayal
Lucky colt,
Covered by garments worn by believing men,
Privileged miracle-watchers of the Master.
Your hooves trod a pavement of cloaks
Thrown before the King.
Lucky colt, sudden transport for the God-Man
Your floppy ears heard praise.
As observers hailed
The Holiness you carried
Upon your humble back.
Lucky colt!

God's Word for You
"Ascribe to the Lord the glory due His name; worship the Lord in the splendor of His holiness." Psalm 29:2

Scary Words

These may be scary words to some:
"The Kingdom will come!"
Anything covered up will be revealed.
All that's hidden will be known.
Things done in the dark will be seen,
Words spoken in privacy will be heard,
Whispers will be loudly proclaimed.

"But do not dread that time." Lord, You say.
"Only fear the one who can hurl humans into hell,
Declare now before men
That you know and worship God
And you will be acknowledged
In the presence of God and the angels."
Lord, what sweet words are these!

God's Word for You
*"For the Lord God is a sun and shield; the Lord
bestows favor and honor..." Psalm 84:11*

Mind's Eye

I see You, Lord, in Samaria at the well.
I can picture You in the Temple.
I visualize You in the desert.
I hear You in the boat.
I hold Your image in my mind.
Always You are:
Father-led,
Spirit-willed,
Heavenly focused.
Walking toward Gethsemane,
Waiting to ride the white horse,
Ready always to act on my behalf,
To love and bless me.

God's Word for You

*"'I give them eternal life, and they shall never perish;
no one can snatch them out of my hand. My Father,
who has given them to me, is greater than all; no one
can snatch them out of my Father's hand. I and the
Father are one'." John 10:28-30*

Lessons

Your disciples thought they had a great idea.
They wanted You to command fire on your enemies.
"Destroy those who refuse to accept You," they
suggested.
But Your plan was to save people from the penalty of
death,
And free them from the distress of sin.
Mercy and grace for all You insisted.
Your disciples had much to learn.
So do I.

God's Word for You
*"Show me Your ways, O Lord, teach me Your paths;
guide me in Your truth and teach me, for you are God
my Savior, and my hope is in You all day long."*
Psalm 25:4

Signs

Lord, You give us signs.
Signs deep with meaning,
Filled with power,
Given for our knowledge.
Sign of the Israelites:
Rebellion leads to strife.
Sign of Jonah:
Disobedience will not be tolerated.
Sign of Mary:
Holiness leads to honor.
Sign of the Pharisees:
Pride leads to false belief.
Sign of Peter:
Impulsiveness leads to error.
Sign of Jesus:
The cross leads to life.
Sign of the Holy Spirit:
Miracles still abound,
Lord, Your signs are clear to me.
Let my life be a sign also,
That others, too, may see.

God's Word for You
"Give me a sign of your goodness, that my enemies may see it and be put to shame, for you, O Lord, have helped me and comforted me." Psalm 86:17

Sowing

The sower sows the Word of God.
It matters not who the sower is.
 The Seed holds the power.
Seed falls on several grounds:
Good,
 Thorn-covered, and
Rocky.
Some seed the sower sows
Holds fast in the ground and
Yields a great crop of fruit.
Some seed the sower sows
Is choked by thorns and withers away.
Some seed the sower sows
 Is smashed by walkers
And eaten by birds.
What waste!
Lord, I pray Your seed
Flourishes in me.

God's Word for You
*"Now he who supplies seed to the sower and bread for
food will also supply and increase your store of seed
and will enlarge the harvest of your righteousness."*
2 Cor 9:10-11

Teacher

Me?
Taught by Jesus?
You, Father, my personal instructor?
Holy Spirit, my Source of Divine Wisdom?
Triune God,
What a huge privilege You give to me!
Eagerly I will listen and learn.

God's Word for You
"For you are great and do marvelous deeds; you alone are God. Teach me your way, O Lord, and I will walk in your truth; give me an undivided heart, that I may fear your name." Psalm 86:10-11

Perfect

Lord, You never do too little,
You never act too late.
Everything You do is perfect,
Perfection personified in reality,
Perfection-made real through Christ.
Although I am unworthy,
Yet You perfect even me,
And create beauty within my imperfect life.

God's Word for You
"He is the Rock, His works are perfect, and all His ways are just. A faithful God who does no wrong, upright and just is He." Deuteronomy 32:4

Life

Lord,
In You,
Through You,
For You.
Lord,
You are the source.
You are the funnel.
You are the filter.
All life comes from You,
Exists through You,
And all life has potential
To move toward completion
In You,
Through You,
For You,
Lord.
So may my life.

God's Word for You
"Find rest, O my soul, in God alone; my hope comes from Him." Psalm 62:4

Chosen

Lord, how can it be
That someone could see You,
And not leave their self-chosen darkness?
Actually hear Your voice,
And still not believe?
How did those who lived at your side
Deny the reality of Your power?
Can the shield of self be so strong
That it will not be penetrated
Even by the very presence of God?
Jesus, You who place spiritual desire within hearts,
And attract those who will come into Your light,
How grateful I am to know You
And rest in the security of being Yours.

God's Word for You

"In him we were also chosen, having been predestined according to the plan of him who works out everything in conformity with the purpose of his will, in order that we, who were the first to hope in Christ, might be for the praise of His glory. And you also were included in Christ when you heard the word of truth, the gospel of your salvation. Having believed, you were marked in Him with a seal, the promised Holy Spirit."
Ephesians 1:11-14

Miracles

I see mini-miracles every day.
The flight of birds.
Squirrel and chipmunks abuzz with chatter.
A sky more exquisite than a Monet.
Mini-miracles abound.

I see major miracles every day, too.
When You allow me to witness
Human "I forgive's" and "I'm sorry's"
Dead souls revitalized with life,
New paths braved with courage.

Miracle-making Lord
Daily You astound me.
Lord, how I love
 Your moments of anointing.
My heart ignites.

The air sizzles.
Senses quicken
Time stops.
Here in this moment
Spirit permeates earth.

God's Word for You
*"But you have an anointing from the Holy One, and
all of you know the truth." 1 John 2:20-21*

Evil

Morning, a new day begins.
I'm fresh and sin-free when I awake.
Streaks of brightness filter through my blinds.
Lord, this awesome interplay of light,
Mixes with shadow on my walls, creates beauty
And makes me ponder the role of darkness.
Is it to emphasize all that's beautiful and bright?

Lord, I'd like it better if sin had no power.
And Satan didn't work so hard to make me cower,
In fact, a world without evil would be fine with me,
But Lord, I know Your plan allow Satan's efforts.
To show me my spiritual might
And strengthen me in doing right.
Is this why you let evil exist?

Both light and darkness interplay within me.
Testing my personality and character,
Yes, I know,
I'm always free to choose how I respond.
Lord, when evening of each day comes,
May I still be beautiful and bright,
And may You be pleased with me.

God's Word for You
"Turn from evil and do good; then you will dwell in the land forever. For the Lord loves the just and will not forsake His faithful ones." Psalm 37:27-28

Sabbath

No work by order
Of the Lord above.
How can it be?
A true Sabbath of rest
An entire twenty-four hours without work!
Lord,
How will I keep my pace?
Don't You know
I need to surge ahead?
How can this be
A holy call
To do no work at all?

A day that's the first of seven,
An opportunity for a glimpse of heaven?
A statute forever You say,
To be observed in every dwelling,
For each generation.
Within every nation.
The Sabbath designed to be a blessing
Lord, it's thoughtful and kind,
I'd like to comply, dare I?
I mean I may fall behind.
What an amazing request
Lord, I'll try.

Beyond Natural

Lord, why?
Why settle for living naturally,
When I can live supernaturally?
Why live worldly,
When I can live unworldly?
Why live thoughtlessly,
When I can live mindfully?
Why settle for less?
Why experience the joys of man,
When I can experience the joys of God?
Why indeed?

Power-Giver

Lord, my Power-giver,
You've implanted strength in me
And given me authority
Over all the firepower of any enemy.
I'm fully equipped to fight,
No battle is beyond reach,
I only need to use the weapons
You've made my own.
Nothing can defeat me,
Not a serpent, scorpion,
 Not condemnation, selfishness.
The enemy will have no victory over me.

God's Word for You
"You give me your shield of victory; You stoop down to make me great. You broaden the path beneath me, so that my ankles do not turn." 2 Samuel 22:36-37

Mysterious Life

Mysterious life,
How long shall it be?

For some it seems too lengthy.
For some too short.
I'm glad You're in charge, Lord, of defining length
And giving occasional extensions,
Like the fifteen years
Faithful Hezekiah received,
Or cutting some lives short
Like haughty Herod.

Lord, how many years
Have you determined for me?
I promise not to rush their use,
But see each day as moments to be lived,
Embracing my challenges and pleasures
As I live fully this mysterious life
For as many years as You've designated
My body shall experience earthly life.

God's Word for You
"Show me, O Lord, my life's end and the number of my days; let me know how fleeting is my life. You have made my days a mere handbreadth; the span of my years is as nothing before you. Each man's life is but a breath." Psalm 39:4-5

Prodigal

Good son, bad son.
Steady son, wandering son.
Content soul, yearning heart,
Lovers of life and joy both,
One son respectful and grateful,
The other callous and unappreciative.
One learned through harsh deprivation,
That stirred memories of warm security
In the place called home.

Good son, bad son,
 Both teach lessons to me.
Two sons equally loved,
Learned to celebrate life,
Appreciate their father,
And express gratitude.
May I do the same.

God's Word for You
"I will declare Your name to my brothers; in the congregation I will praise You." Psalm 22:22

Temple

Lord, how appalling!
The sacred temple
Turned into a hangout for buying and selling.
Your house of holiness for all the nations,
Transformed into a roost for robbers!
The temple enclosure made into a traffic short cut!

The multitude was struck with astonishment
At your strong reaction,
Driving forth the desecrators
And instilling fear in the chief priests,
Who had allowed these violations.
Good for you, Lord!

Lord, I too guard a holy temple,
May I keep sacred my physical body,
This Holy Spirit dwelling place,
Pure of defilement always.
May my body forever be
Worthy of your presence.

God's Word for You
"Don't you know that you yourselves are God's temple and God's spirit lives in you? For God's temple is sacred and you are that temple."
1 Corinthians 3:16, 17

Royalty

Lord, You've made me in effect a princess,
Married to a conquering prince.
Together we reign with authority
Over our home, Your Kingdom on earth.
We bow before You, triumphant King.
We're united in spirit in the throne room of God.
Our children have a heritage of royalty,
Thanks to You, dear Lord!
How awesome that You've given us
These sons and daughters to teach and guide.
Your princes and princesses
Shall dine daily at our side.
Help us remember each meal is a sacred time
An interlude for training and loving
These little lords and ladies You've sent to our home.
May we be mindful Lord and tender and wise
It's a mighty role.
Parenting is the greatest work we can do.
Children are imperfect in their natural state,
Yet eager and willing to learn.
You've made us royal models, they're ready to follow.
Help us, Lord,
These royal youth must be raised well
To become responsible and holy for their King.

God's Word for You
"But you are a chosen people, a royal priesthood, a holy nation, a people belonging to God, that you may declare the praises of him who called you out of darkness into his wonderful light." 1 Peter 2:9-10

Pharisees

The Pharisees engaged in watching You Lord,
And studying Your actions, as they stalked You.
They sifted through Your words.

Perfection of God, You became man's prey.
Pharisees' questions emanated from twisted tongues.
These self-seekers didn't know what to make of
selfless love.

Satan played the religious leaders for fools,
But their deed of darkness and death
Could hold You, Lord, only three days.

Before the Spirit set You free.
Then the empty tomb revealed undeniable truth.
Jesus, fully God, walked the earth again for all to see.

Generation after generation has come.
The man the Pharisees wanted to destroy,
The humble Son of God, lives!

God's Word for You
"Woe to you, teachers of the law and Pharisees, you hypocrites! You are like whitewashed tombs, which look beautiful on the outside but on the inside are full of dead men's bones and everything unclean...on the inside you are full of hypocrisy and wickedness."
Matthew 23:27-28

Kingdom

Lord,
I think, finally,
I understand.

Thy kingdom come
Means
My Kingdom must go.

Thy Way, Lord
Means
Not choosing my own fruitless paths.

Thy Will, Lord
Means
My ego cannot reign.

Cease endless striving
Means
Live a truly happy life.

Lord,
It's so simple
Why do I struggle?

Seek Your kingdom first,
That's the way.
Help me live it.

God's Word for You

"He replied, 'The knowledge of the secrets of the kingdom of heaven has been given to you, but not to them. Whoever has will be given more, and he will have an abundance. Whoever does not have, even what he has will be taken from him.'"
Matthew 13:11-12

Authority

Lord, while upon this earth,
You called Yourself
A fire starter,
A division-maker.
A unity-restorer.
A peace-giver,
A peace-breaker,
A rule-changer,
A new priority-maker,
A Kingdom-creator.

Heavy tasks for a mighty hand
And a holy heart.
Works fit for one alone -
The amazing, the only,
The beloved,
Son of God
And now Lord,
You've made Your authority mine.
And commissioned me to use it well.

God's Word for You
"Great is the Lord and most worthy of praise; His greatness no one can fathom." Psalm 145:3

Mount Olivet

Lord, many nights at the Mount called Olivet,
Before the fateful night of Your betrayal,
Were quiet times of rest after teaching in the temple
courts
But evenings of turmoil, too,
Because of Your knowledge of what lie ahead,
Your soon-coming agony.

It had to be hard to think of anything else,
Yet You did, and planned my future lessons,
Preparing the way for me at this holy place called
Olivet.
Through your actions soon to be recorded in four
gospels.

Lord, I, too, have lessons to teach now
As I dwell on my own Mount Olivet.

God's Word for You
*"The Lord is faithful to all His promises and loving
toward all He has made. The Lord upholds all those
who fall and lifts up all who are bowed down."*
Psalm 145:13b, 14

Apparel

Lord, Me?
You've issued me
An invitation to heaven,
To everlasting, sacred joy!

Lord, I accept!
However since, as You know
I don't have the right apparel,
I shall slip into the glowing garment
Of holiness You've provided.
Now tell me please,
What gifts should I bring?

Only invisible gifts
Like trust and obedience?
Oh Lord, my Gracious Host,
Let the celebration begin!

God's Word for You
"Those who are far from You will perish; you destroy all who are unfaithful to You. But as for me, it is good to be near God. I have made the Sovereign Lord my refuge." Psalm 73:27, 28

Temptation

The key to conquest has been revealed,
Recorded for all generations,
Slipped in the account of the Lord's prayer.
Victory over sin can be mine.
A simple, powerful command,
"Pray that you may not enter into temptation."

Lord, that is truly my desire,
The secret to victory as stated in the Our Father.
But often I slip into pettiness,
Flirt with bitterness and
Find myself failing to be kind.

Lord, deliver me from such temptations every day!

God's Word for You
"I know your deeds. See, I have placed before you an open door no one can shut. I know that you have little strength, yet you have kept my word and have not denied my name." Revelation 3:8

Fullness of Joy

Today and every day Lord, You say:

"I will be your God,
I will be your life."

"Celebrate and dance,
The fullness of joy is here."

Dear God can this be true?
A life of constant joy is pleasing to You?

Dance and twirl with joy?
What about cross-carrying and fasting?

"These too have a place," You say,
"But they never were meant to take away joy."

Oh Lord, laughter floods my heart,
That You would allow such delight!

The fullness of joy!
Hallelujah!

God's Word for You
"I will sing and make music with all my soul."
Psalm 108:1b

Cup

Angel from heaven,
You strengthened the Spirit of Jesus,
Often, I, too, become weak.
Lord, send an angel to me.
My cup is not of death, yet difficult all the same.
Lord, the more agony you experienced,
The more intently and earnestly You prayed.
You asked for Your cup's removal,
Yet seeking always not Your will, but Abba's.
I, too, pray to the Father.
Angel from heaven come,
Make me strong enough
To drink from my cup.

God's Word for You
"Who shall separate us from the love of Christ? Shall trouble or hardship or persecution or famine or nakedness or danger or sword? As it is written: For your sake we face death all day long; we are considered as sheep to be slaughtered. No, in all these things we are more than conquerors through him who loved us." Romans 8:34-37

Sea Watch

Lord, even after the miracle meal for 5000,
Your disciples experienced fear
In the rocky boat on the stormy lake.
When You walked on that raging sea to reach them.
They were astonished that You came.

Because their hearts were dull,
They failed to understand
The teaching and meaning
Of Your miraculous dinner for thousands.
Lord, how could they be so dense?

Lord, how can I be so foolish?
Why do I so soon forget
That Your care is constant?
Your watchfulness over me never ceases.
I'm grateful that You respond to my every need.

God's Word for You
"You hold me by my right hand. You guide me with Your counsel, and afterward You will take me into glory."
Psalm 73:23b, 24

Extravagance

Lord, dinner leftovers didn't bother You.
Not even twelve baskets full,
You always produced enough,
And often blessed with more.

You are an extravagant God,
Giver beyond measure.
The fruit of the fields are more feast than birds can eat,
The blessings I experience are more than I can fathom.

Giver extraordinaire,
May I be generous with your same measure.
Open my fist that sometimes clings too tight,
That I may model Your extravagance.

God's Word for You
"When they had all had enough to eat, he [Jesus] said to his disciples, "Gather the pieces that are left over. Let nothing be wasted. So they gathered them and filled twelve baskets with the pieces of the five barley loaves left over by those who had eaten."
John 6:12-13

Signals

Persistent pain,
Signals of physical or spiritual distress
Insistently demand correction
It's horrid to endure physical discomfort
Or spiritual agony,
How pain hurts!
Oh for surcease and freedom!
I recall with longing my past moments
Not marred by such intrusion.
Twinges of conscience, stabs of guilt
Systems alert,
 Do something, relieve the body,
Heal the soul.
Freedom from pain
Is my only aim.
Lord, may I heed the signals,
Endure the travail,
Read the message pain tells
And be restored to health and holiness.

God's Word for You
*"Not only so, but we also rejoice in our sufferings,
because we know that suffering produces perseverance;
perseverance, character; and character, hope."*
Romans 5:3-5

Opinion

The opinion of others used to mean much
An approval-seeker was I.
Since I accepted the work of the cross,
I consider the Lord's opinion alone.

Put me on trial.
Investigate me.
Question me.
I'm blameless.

The Lord has already examined and acquitted me.
He knows my aims,
Understands my motives,
Forgives my sins.

I trust His judgment completely.
With all due respect.
Human opinion means little to me,
Lord what a gift! You've made me free.

God's Word for You
"In God whose word I praise, in God I trust, I will not be afraid. What can mortal man do to me? All day long they twist my words. They are always plotting against me." Psalm 56:4-5

Commander-in-Chief

Lord, awesome commander,
Great war strategist,
Battle-wise beyond the skill of man,
You used simple weapons,
Empty pitchers with torches within,
Trumpet sounds that destroyed fortifications,
To lead Your people to victory.
You defeated an army with a parted sea,
No feat is too great after You train me.
Lord, I'm honored to be your soldier,
Ready for combat, I await your orders
And Your sweet power
To accomplish Your every purpose.

God's Word for You
"See, I am setting before you today a blessing and a curse the blessing if you obey the commands of the LORD your God that I am giving you today; the curse if you disobey the commands of the LORD your God and turn from the way that I command you today by following other gods." Deuteronomy 11:26-28

Hiding Places

Hiding places:
Isolation,
Busyness,
Depression,
Anger.
Withdrawal begins with ease.
It seems safe,
But it's a place of danger.
"Come out of hiding," Lord, You say.
"You need not hide,
You have My power,
Now use it!"
Lord, You say:
"Remember, dear ones,
You can feel depressed
When I test you,
You can feel oppressed,
When you choose to disobey me.
Know I will chastise and guide you.
Not to constrain you,
But to train you.
When Satan seeks to swarm over you,
Don't run to a hiding place,
Come to Me,
The only safe place."

God's Word for You
"You are my hiding place; You will protect me from trouble and surround me with songs of deliverance." Psalm32:7

One Alone

My soul waits in silence,
In supreme submission to One alone,
The Lord is my high tower of protection.
I have confidence in God each moment,
The Rock Who keeps me immovable.
I will lift up my hands in Your name.

To You I cling.
Lord, You are the One true God,
Great source of every expectation.
My inner self longs for You
And yearns to see Your power and glory.
I wait with upraised hands
And lips moving in praise.

God's Word for You
"I have seen you in the sanctuary and beheld your power and your glory. Because your love is better than life, my lips will glorify you." Psalm 63:2-3

Trickster

The enemy's' job,
Mighty trickster,
Is to make you believe you're defeated,
And frighten you into thinking
He has authority over you,
But your bondage is unnecessary.

Let God's Word to Gideon
Ring true for you:
"The Lord is with you."

Gideon named his altar,
 "The altar of peace."
So, life can be for you,
Let your turmoil cease.

No trickster can deceive you,
You have victory in God.

God's Word for You
*"But I call to God, and the Lord saves me. Evening,
morning and noon I cry out in distress, and He hears
my voice." Psalm 57:16,17*

Worship

Lord, worship is sometimes a challenge.
I struggle to give my mind fully,
Help me please, for I know,
You despise careless, irreverent worship
And find no pleasure in the half-attention of fools.
You desire worship filled with praise that leads to
action
And cares for the needs of the oppressed.

True worship persists regardless of circumstances
Even in periods of enduring sadness.

Lord, guard me from the ruin
That comes from failing to draw near to hear,
From thoughtless words and acts,
And a mind given to wandering.
May my sacrifice of worship be nothing less than all
of myself.
I desire to be fully present in honoring You
And celebrating the love You've given.

God's Word for You
"I will praise You forever for what You have done; in Your name I will hope, for Your name is good. I will praise You in the presence of Your saints." Psalm 52:9

Book of Life

God's book of life is written,
The record of God's own,
The book of the living,
The one and only book of life.

The book of life will be used to judge
What the living and the dead have done,
Their feelings, thoughts, and acts,
Will be recorded there forever.

Praise you Jesus,
Warrior in white,
I await the opening of your book.
More than anything I desire to be with you.

The book lists the names of the upright
In good standing with God.
God, You have promised deliverance
To everyone whose name is written there.

These shall walk with God in white
Because they are deserving and worthy.
Their names will never be blotted out.
Lord, I praise You that my name is there.

Desire

Wants, needs and desire,
How they frolic together.
Only one is essential,
Yet they're difficult to sort,
Unless I go deep within
Strip away my selfish motives,
And stifle my human pride.
Show me truth, Lord,
About my dreams and goals,
As I am in pursuit of both.
Tell me Your plans, Lord,
For how my hopes are to be met.
Draw me close to your side,
When I must wait or do without.

Lord, for each need met,
Each granted desire,
Every undeserved gift,
I thank you.

"May He give you the desire of your heart and make all your plans succeed. We will shout for joy when you are victorious and will lift up our banners in the name of our God. May the Lord grant all your requests."
Psalm 20:4-5

Either - Or

Either predestined,
Or post-destined?
Either pre-trib,
Or post-trib?
These either / ors
Matter not at all.
The only either-or of real significance is
Eternal salvation or damnation.
Rejecting God,
Or accepting the love of God.
Choosing to trust God,
And I do.

God's Word for You
"But I am like an olive tree flourishing in the house of God; I trust in God's unfailing love for ever and ever."
Psalm 52:8

Stories

The book of God holds the stories of many lives.
Tales about kings and peasants,
Kings who were sinners with sons who were saints.
Stories of the rich and royal
And the poor and unnamed,
Weak, unwise youth and smart ones, too.
Parables about pearls and yeast and seeds
Dramas to be recalled forever.
Samson's hair,
Gideon's torches of triumph,
Job's disasters.

Such stories make me mindful
Of another story that unfolds.
How will my life story read?
I'd like a happy story Lord,
A love story, a success story,
But I know that's not always possible.
Most important how shall my story end?
May it be a good ending, please Father,
 Embraced in your arms.
Until then keep me safe, Lord,
Content whatever my circumstances.

God's Word for You
*"If they obey and serve him, they will spend the rest of
their days in prosperity and their years in
contentment." Job 36:11*

Control

Lord, You have clear expectations for me.
I am to live with inner calm,
And control my response to situations.
Your command is clear.
I am not to let myself get agitated,
Quit allowing myself to feel unsettled,
And refuse to worry.
Lord, why is this so hard?

Lord, I'd hoped You'd do it all.
Life would be much easier that way.
But, You say I have a role to play.
I must admit it surprises me,
That I have this much control.
Yet, I do, You insist, Lord.

I am not to allow myself to feel intimidated,
I must reject cowardice,
Be fearless in every challenge.
You always give me the power I need,
Now I must use it with Your help.
 At times it seems impossible,
Yet, Lord, I will try.

God's Word for You
"So do not fear, for I am with you; do not be dismayed, for I am your God. I will strengthen you and help you; I will uphold you with my righteous right hand." Isaiah 41:10

Origin

Mankind, created or evolved?
The question of our origin hovers.
Planned or happenstance?
The evolutionists tangled web of assumptions
Without scientific strength,
Has made for interesting conjecture,
Often filled with misconception.
Missing links have never been found.

Now science has revealed patterns,
Intricate DNA in genetic structure,
Electron microscopes, computer time projections,
These provide undeniable evidence.
Evolution is untenable, unfathomable.
Man was created purposely by God, for God.

God's Word for You
"So God created mankind in his own image, in the image of God he created them; male and female he created them." Genesis 1:27

Folly

The message of the cross of Christ
Is considered by many sheer folly,
Unreasonable to intelligent minds,
Even to the point of being absurd
To those heading toward perdition.

But the very opposite is true
Folly lies with those who deny its message.
God has destroyed
The cleverness of the clever,
The learning of the learned,
The philosophy of the philosophers.
Foolish is all the world's wisdom,
Nonsense even,
That doesn't recognize the message of God.

The cross may appear folly,
To those who deny it,
But Christ crucified
Is the exquisite wisdom of God.

God's Word for You
*"Therefore once more I will astound these people with
wonder upon wonder; the wisdom of the wise will
perish, the intelligence of the intelligent will vanish."*
Isaiah 29:14

Energy

Lord, this passion,
Spirit-stirred in my soul by You,
I cannot begin to describe
The energy You give.
You make each day a wonder
Filled with unfolding miracles.
Life exudes through Your Spirit.
I love to sense You near
And realize to my amazement
You delight in using me for Your glory.

God's Word for You
"I will come down and speak with you there, and I will take some of the power of the Spirit that is on you and put it on them. They will share the burden of the people with you so that you will not have to carry it alone."
Numbers 11:17

Covenant

The covenant with our God,
Old and new,
Is still valid today.
This amazes me.
Lord, You'd do for me
What You did for the Israelites
In the days of Joshua.
You've given me a country to live in
For which I did not labor
And cities and towns which I did not build.
I eat from fields I did not plant.
Your covenant of love
Meets my every need.
All that's Yours is mine You say.
If I will forsake idols that can still attract
And serve You alone.
Lord, my choice is made,
To live in covenant with You
With all my heart.

God's Word for You
*"Now fear the Lord and serve him with all faithfulness.
Joshua 24:13-14*

Reality

Lord, death comes to all.
I know the fact well,
But intellectually I can't comprehend
That death is coming for me.
Someday I will walk this earth no more.
At that time I pray
There are no past wrongs I neglected to right.
May this reality of death pierce my mind
And influence well my thoughts and actions.
With the Psalmist David I want to say
"I will bless You, Lord, while I live.
For You are my ever-present help,
My joy in life and hope in death."
I will praise you as long as I live,
and in your name I will lift up my hands.
Lord, keep me ready,
And help me remember:
"Eye has not seen,
Nor ear heard the wonders
God has prepared for those who love Him."
This is truth.
This is reality.

God's Word for You
"There is no one like the God of Jeshurun, who rides across the heavens to help you and on the clouds in his majesty." Deuteronomy 33:26

Great Stone

Great stone,
Set in place by Joshua.
Under the oak tree
As witness to the people.
And as a sign in the Word for me.
Great stone
In the court of the Lord's sanctuary
On the day Joshua made a covenant
Reminding the people always
Lest they forget
Or later lie and deny that they agreed
To incline their hearts to the Lord,
"The Lord our God we will serve;
His voice we will obey."
Great stone – strong witness.
Little stone set in my garden plot.
Reminds me of my covenant also
To serve the Lord with all my heart forever.

God's Word for You
"And Joshua recorded these things in the Book of the Law of God. Then he took a large stone and set it up there under the oak near the holy place of the Lord."
Joshua 24:26

Rest

Lord, people keep coming and going.
Those close to me,
And some I scarcely know.
I need a deserted place.
Show me please a solitary spot.
The strain of people and hectic thoughts
Gives peace no space.

Help me find a slower mental pace.
Lord, Shepherd, lead me to such a place.
Within or without my body I care not,
Only please guide me to rest,
That I may be replenished by You.
Lord, where shall I go?
Lead me there.

God's Word for You
"But now the Lord my God has given me rest on every side, and there is no adversary or disaster."
1Kings 5:4

Seventy-Two

Oh Lord, what 72 can do,
Empowered by You!
72 drove out evil spirits
And healed the sick
With nothing for the journey.
Save a walking stick.
No food, no money, no extra clothes.
But sandals to be used for dust-shaking
For any community that refused
To welcome any two of the 72.
72 equipped with cloaks and walking sticks
Gives me cause to ponder.

I have more tools to use:
Churches, Bible studies,
Christian books, periodicals,
Fellowship groups, retreats.
But do they sometimes get in the way
Of doing what the 72 did?
72 men willing to tell all about You,
Loving people to You wherever they went.
Lord, may I move in my world
With the confidence and power of these 72.
And forgive me when I forget my holy mission
To fill the shoes of these 72.

Peace

A sense of peacefulness eludes me
Midst my afflictions and disturbances
Where shall I find sweet peace?

Within my spirit of course,
As I go before the throne.
Lord, I wait. Speak.

Fill me with Your Spirit.
That I may exude Your presence.
And share Your truth everywhere.

Shepherd

Lord, teacher of wondrous concepts,
Multiplier of loaves and fishes,
Satisfier of bodies and souls.
Restorer of health
Giver to all who approached You,
Whatever their need.

I delight in knowing
I too have You as my shepherd,
Diligent and watchful,
And You will do for me
What you've done for others.
You care for sheep and I am One.

God's Word for You
"The Lord is my shepherd, I lack nothing. He makes me lie down in green pastures, he leads me beside quiet waters, he refreshes my soul. He guides me along the right paths for his name's sake." Psalm 23: 1-3

Pretenders

Pharisees,
Pretenders,
Hypocrites
You put on a nice show,
Honoring God with your lips,
But holding Your heart far off
And staying distant from God.
Worshipping Him showily,
While remaining without joy,
Clinging to the tradition of men,
Telling others to observe God's Commandments,
While doing as you please.
Murmuring against His truth,
You idolized human forefathers
And savored your brief human power.
Pretenders, hypocrites!
Roast in Gehanna.
Do not blame God.
The decision is yours.
The decision is mine.

God's Word for You
"Then they understood that he was not telling them to guard against the yeast used in bread, but against the teaching of the Pharisees and Sadducees."
Matthew 16:12

Man of Sorrows

Lord, Man of sorrows they called You,
When they wounded You for my wrongs,
Chastised You without cause to attain my good.
You were wounded by whip straps,
Silent before your tormentors
So that I could sing forever.
Holder of all the world's guilt
Carrier of my iniquities
You secured my healings and wholeness.
You who had no sin assumed mine.
How could You do this for me?

God's Word for You
"But Jesus remained silent and gave no answer. Again the high priest asked him, 'Are you the Messiah, the Son of the Blessed One?'" Mark 14:61

Easy and Hard

Being "saved" is simple,
Living the saved life is a challenge,
Declaring the truth of the Word of God is easy,
Applying it to my life is hard.
Being in community is comfortable
Interacting lovingly with unlovables isn't.
Tending to the needs of others is a challenge.
Experiencing God's love is simple,
Living totally confident of His love isn't.
The Christian life is joy and test.
Easy and hard,
Hard and easy,
The challenge is great.

God's Word for You
"The Lord is my strength and my defense; He has become my salvation. He is my God, and I will praise him, my father's God, and I will exalt him."
Exodus 15:2

Passion

Lord, the passion I feel for You
 Has no bounds,
The union of my soul with Yours
Is strong.

You are the solitary force,
That attracts and drives me.
With you I ride a cloud
And wing among the stars.

My throat aches each day
As I gaze upon Your creation
Until I voice my praise,
For Your miracles never fail to amaze.

Lord, to say the words "I love You,"
Sound far too ordinary,
For my God so extraordinary!
Lord, I long to honor You with all I am.

God's Word for You
"For this is what the high and exalted One says— he who lives forever, whose name is holy: 'I live in a high and holy place, but also with the one who is contrite and lowly in spirit, to revive the spirit of the lowly and to revive the heart of the contrite.'"
Isaiah 57:15

Word Limits

Lord,
Words, words, words,
Often say nothing,
Mean little, and
Fail to capture the essence
Of what is meant.
Words are of limited use
To describe You, My limitless God.
Words only occasionally touch the reality
Of Who You are.
Yet words are my only tool
To express Your holiness
And reveal Your majesty.

Words can describe Your desire for my best
I used to live like my best is yet to be.
But I've come to see
The best is this well-lived moment.
When I add my simple faith, hope and charity to it.
It's important to perfect these qualities
Then the rest of life can come naturally
Even supernaturally.
When I focus on Your best Lord.
With praise for every moment.

God's Word for You
"You must present as the Lord's portion the best and holiest part of everything given to you." Numbers 18:29

Acceptance

Lord, I'd like to keep part of my life as it is,
And have You change the rest
Picking and choosing what I think best.
I like Your will, I want it of course,
But only the parts that fits my plans,
And could I skip the tests?

Lord, okay!
Have Your way.
I promise not to grumble,
But please don't let me stumble.
I easily could You know,
Sometimes I fail to see
The good You've planned for me.

God's Word for You
"And I, the Lord, because of their actions and imaginations, am about to come and gather all nations and tongues, and they will come and see my glory."
Isaiah 66:18

The Grip

Lord, You gripped the twelve-year-old hand firmly,
Of the young girl You snatched from death.
Instantly she was up and walking about.
The journey from death back to life
Leaves a girl hungry.
You thought of everything.
And suggested she be given something to eat,
Lest her joy-filled parents forget.
You told them to tell no one
About their daughter's return to life.
You wanted her protected
From people who might badger and question.
After all what could she say but
I was lifeless,
Now I walk and breathe.
Her father, the synagogue ruler,
Had been powerless to help,
Yet wise enough to seek out
The miracle-working Son of God.
Lord, I, too, was dead,
Lifted by Your grip,
Now I live victoriously
To celebrate You,
My supreme life-giver.

God's Word for You
"Immediately the girl stood up and began to walk around (she was twelve years old). At this they were completely astonished." Mark 5:42

Sin

Lord, how to describe sin?
Sin is like entering darkness,
While thinking I'm seeing something bright,
Desiring what won't make me happy,
Deciding to do what I shouldn't,
Entering a doorway to loss,
Walking a path to ultimate misery.

Lord, how powerfully sin attracts!
This instrument of Satan fools so well.
Looking attractive, seemingly good,
Then snatching away my self-respect
And searing my soul.
Satan sneers the second I succumb.
Lord, please keep me aware of sin's ploys.
I pray I'll sin no more.

God's Word for You
"When anyone becomes aware that they are guilty in any of these matters, they must confess in what way they have sinned." Leviticus 5:5

Temples

Lord, this business of religion wearies me.
Building churches, for whom and how much?
Holding committee meetings,
Handling disagreements.
I'm sure a certain amount must go on,
But I fear the business proceeds to excess
And worship time often becomes less and less.

Lord, Your method seems best.
You formed a training group of twelve
With only one temple in each town for all.
You wanted Your message shared
 Within one community of believing hearts.
Lord, might there be too many physical temples,
Called churches today,
And too few spiritual ones?

God's Word for You
"Nevertheless, each person should live as a believer in whatever situation the Lord has assigned to them, just as God has called them. This is the rule I lay down in all the churches." 1 Corinthians 7:17

Spirit

Holy Spirit, how I'd like to have been there
When You appeared to that terrified group
Assembled fearfully in the upper room.

I'd like to experience the sound from heaven,
And the sight of tongues resembling flames of fires
Separated and settling on each person.

Oh to hear the music of many languages
Pouring from those tongues,
Telling everyone of the greatness of God!

Holy Spirit, fully present here and now,
Create the same fire and music again in me.
Diffuse it throughout my soul.

Let observers be beside themselves
Again today as at the first Pentecost,
That all may exalt You and Your mighty works.

God's Word for You
"They saw what seemed to be tongues of fire that separated and came to rest on each of them." Acts 2:3

Clear Signs

Lord, how can I know for sure
People who are truly Yours?
Christians not in mere name,
But by life choices?
What shall I look for?
Gladness,
Simplicity,
Generosity,
Steadfastness,
Heartfelt Praise,
Single Purpose,
Unfailing Integrity,
Acceptance of the Father's will.
Yes, these will do.
Lord, You say:
"They are clear signs of
Those who are Mine.
Not servants to things,
But servants to Me, the King of Kings."

God's Word for You
*"I charge you to keep this command without spot or
blame until the appearing of our Lord Jesus Christ,
which God will bring about in his own time—God,
the blessed and only Ruler, the King of kings and
Lord of lords." 1 Timothy 6:15*

Meeting

Lord, You liked to wake up early
And hurry off into the hills.

The exciting lure
Of being alone with Your father
Pulled You from sleep
And drew You from the presence
Of Your beloved disciples.
I too feel the same pull as my eyes meet morning
And I rush to our meeting place.

Lord, You became energized for Your day
In the renewing presence of Your Papa.

I wonder what Your earthly life would have been,
If You'd neglected this morning meeting.
I know how crazy and fruitless my days are
When I fail to be alone in Your presence.
Help me remember when my bed seems too sweet,
The precious, lasting benefit of being with You
Far outweighs the brief pleasure of sleep.

God's Word for You
*"In those days Jesus went out to the mountain to pray,
and He spent the night in prayer to God." Luke 6:12*

Paul

Paul, you were blinded in an instant,
Frightened beyond belief,
And then able to see.
God-struck, You absorbed the shock.
What an extraordinary event this had to be.

The Lord asked,
"Why Saul, do you persecute Me."
And your allegiance changed forever.
Never again would Christianity seem false
To You who declared, "For me to live is Christ."

Trouble came fast and furious then.
Physical bondage became frequent
Yet you lived each moment joyfully.
Your hope never wavered
In the Christ who set You free.

I have your conviction, Paul,
I need your courage.

God's Word for You
*"Immediately there fell from his eyes something like
scales, and he received his sight at once, and he arose
and was baptized." Acts 9:18*

Fire and Faith

Persistent faith,
Faith like fire
Spreading everywhere
Good fire, warming fire, healing fire.
Holy Spirit tongues-licking fire.

Scripture fire,
Fire safe for walking through
Without being burned.
Fire burning spontaneously for Elijah,
Demonstrating God's power.

Bad fire,
Doubt, rebellion fire,
Lack of faith, killing fire,
Destroying fire,
Fire of hell that can't be quenched.

Holy fire,
Spirit fire,
Burn bright in me forever.
Keep me glowing before man,
Blazing with faith in God.

God's Word for You
"'As for me, this is my covenant with them,' says the Lord. 'My Spirit, who is on you, will not depart from you, and my words that I have put in your mouth will always be on your lips, on the lips of your children and on the lips of their descendants—from this time on and forever,' says the Lord." Isaiah 59:21

Evangelists

Matthew, Mark, Luke and John,
Did you ever think you'd be so famous?
Millions of copies of your Gospels
Are scattered around the world.
How delightful to think you never knew or cared.

Because it wasn't about fame, was it?
Nor about numbers who heard,
But only following His will.
Spurred by compulsion
Born of love.

You felt compelled to record
The work of the One
Who led you to the Father.
So may I,
So may we all.

God's Word for You
"This is all I want to ask of you: did you receive the [Holy] Spirit as the result of obeying [the requirements of] the Law, or was it the result of hearing [the message of salvation and] with faith [believing it]?" Galatians 3:2

Simple Faith

Lord, you touched the children one by one,
Placing Your holy hands of blessing upon them
And scolded the disciples who would keep
These little ones away.
Fervently You prayed for each child
And admired aloud the simple faith
Of those who eagerly accepted You
And welcomed Your kingdom
With total delight.

Lord, like a little child may I be,
Fully embracing every encounter with You
And welcoming Your plans for me,
Day by day, minute by minute.

God's Word for You
*"People were bringing little children to Jesus for him
to place his hands on them, but the disciples rebuked
them. When Jesus saw this, he was indignant. He said
to them, "Let the little children come to me, and do not
hinder them, for the kingdom of God belongs to such
as these" Mark 10:13-16.*

Gloom and Grief

Gloom and grief followed
The rich, young man who walked away from Jesus
Clutching great possessions,
But abandoning heaven's treasures.

Gloom and grief became his companions,
Rather than the joy and delight
Jesus desired to lavish.
The young man's decision seemed unwise.

But how often do I covet material stuff
And fall for Satan's line
Holding tightly even mental possessions
Like guilt, bitterness, and revenge?

How foolishly I abandon my true delight,
Disrupting my peace and freedom
Losing the treasure of a holy, clear mind
Allowing gloom and grief to invade me.

A joy-filled Kingdom can be mine,
If I stay under Jesus' command.
Gloom and grief be gone,
I shall live mindful of heavenly priorities.

God's Word for You
"But whoever drinks the water that I give him will never be thirsty again. But the water that I give him will become in him a spring of water welling up to eternal life." John 4:14

Whole Heart

With all my heart,
All my soul,
All my life force,
All my mind,
All my strength
Physical,
Emotional,
Spiritual
With all I am.

So will I love You.
Oh Lord,
My God.
So will I serve You,
Oh Lord,
My God.
So will I glorify You,
Oh Lord,
My God.

God's Word for You
"For where your treasure is, there your heart will be also." Matthew 6:21

Down and Up

I'm down, Lord.
The work is hard.
I'm bruised by the
World's pressures
And the devil's thrusts.
My flesh wants to quit.
Come lift my head,
Renew my strength,
Soothe my heart.
Be quick, I pray.
Help me make a fresh start
Of this new day.
I open Your Word for encouragement.
Knowing no Word of God is without power.
And no word of Yours goes unfulfilled.
Living Word, loving Word,
Incomparable Word of God.
I read, I ponder,
I'm hope-filled again.

God's Word for You
"For the word of God is alive and active. Sharper than any double-edged sword, it penetrates even to dividing soul and spirit, joints and marrow; it judges the thoughts and attitudes of the heart." Hebrews 4:12

Responses

Glorious Lord,
Restorer of Health,
Keeper of Truth
Maker of Men,
How I like to imagine, Lord,
The responses You stirred.
What did these people think --
The leper who was embraced,
The boys who'd known death suddenly alive,
The Roman soldier once trained to bow to Caesar
Overcome with allegiance to a new master.
The old woman overjoyed in giving all,
The young woman freed
Who'd been captive to seeking phony love for coins.
What did they think, I wonder?
Did praise simply burst from their souls,
Resplendent, magnificent, full of delight?
Did heads drop, knees bend?
How I like to imagine, Lord,
The responses You stirred.

God's Word for You
"Jesus went through all the towns and villages, teaching in their synagogues, proclaiming the good news of the kingdom and healing every disease and sickness." Matthew 9:35

Two

Incarnation.
Two natures,
God – Man
Never before has there been,
Or ever could be again,
One person in the flesh,
Another in the spirit.
Natural plus supernatural spirit.
Invisible God,
Visible man.
Two natures,
A mystery of enormous importance,
Love and life unfolding.
Human being extraordinaire,
Yet always:
One will alone— The Father's.

God's Word for You
"For in Him the whole fullness of deity dwells bodily."
Colossians 2:9

Soul Ablaze

Lord, You've set my soul ablaze
By touching it to Yours,
I revel in Your warmth,
And bask in the flame of Your presence.

I don't want to leave the hearth
Where the love fire roars.
Is that how it was for You
When You went from heaven to earth?

Yet, Lord, You send me forth
With burning coals - truth and love -
To ignite the dryness around me
With eternal embers that glow forever.

For You desire to set more souls ablaze
With fire that heals and purifies,
Supernatural flames that create rather than destroy
Spreading with power through this parched world.

Lord, I will be Your torch,
I'll run the race for You.
One thing alone I ask -
Keep me ablaze with Your truth and love.

God's Word for You
"What does the Lord your God ask of you but to fear the Lord your God, to walk in obedience to him, to love him, to serve the Lord your God with all your heart and with all your soul." Deuteronomy 10:12

Thanks

I begin this new day,
Telling You, my great Lord,
How grateful I am
For my gift of life,
For plans You've directed,
For Your many awesome healings,
For keeping safe those I love.
For giving me a competent mind
 That comprehends Who You are,
And understands who I am in You.
You've made me fire-born for Spirit work,
Designed by You for this day, this time.
Thank You, my great Lord.

God's Word for You
"But you are a chosen people, a royal priesthood, a holy nation, God's special possession, that you may declare the praises of him who called you out of darkness into his wonderful light." 1 Peter 2:9

Crosses

Crosses, crosses everywhere.
Metal crosses with clean, sharp lines,
Wooden crosses with carved, intricate symbols,
Crosses of ceramic, collectors of dust on walls,
Whose owners have ceased to see them.
Ornamental crosses hanging around necks
Filled with meaning or meaningless?
Invisible crosses carried throughout lives
With dignity and determination.
Holy crosses that serve as reminders
Of one sacred cross carried
And a precious life sacrificed --
The cross that made kingdom dwellers
Of common people like you and me,
Because God was glorified upon it.
The cross that brought grace to the world
Enables me to carry my crosses with confidence.

God's Word for You
"Therefore we do not lose heart. Though outwardly we are wasting away…" 2 Corinthians 4:16

Trinity

Father, Son, Spirit,
Love, love, love.
Three words,
Three Persons in One God.
All three in love with Me!
Triune God, I'm in awe,
As I contemplate Your existence.
Triune God, trice sovereign,
Triple goodness.
Help my mind comprehend
The reality of this mystery.
My desire is strong, but
My reason struggles.
Sharpen my senses.
Enhance my awareness
That I may properly honor
The treasure and truth of Trinity,
My beloved Triune God.

God's Word for You
"I have not departed from the commands of his lips; I have treasured the words of his mouth more than my daily bread." Job 23:12

Healing

Health failed me,
Hope seemed to elude me,
Then I beseeched You.

I waited.
It seemed too long,
For my ill, impatient body.

But in the rightness of time.
You answered anew.
You restored my hope.

Emotionally and physically,
You bandaged my hurts
With spiritual silk.

Banished my terror
With touches of Your hand,
And made me well again.

Lord, I praise You!
Amazing healing God,
I can never thank you enough!

God's Word for You
"Heal me, Lord, and I will be healed; save me and I will be saved, for You are the One I praise."
Jeremiah 17:14

Eden Glimpses

Lord, it seems I must in Eden be,
I awake on a summer morn in the Gardens.
Forest birds chatter greetings to the new day,
Conferencing excitedly over their territories.
Deep red berries highlight the forest greenery.
Purple spirea and haughty hydrangea
Adorn nature's canvas.

Squirrels hold court
Over intruding chipmunks.
Deer with fawns prance through the woods
Heralding their freedom.

Natural life abounds
In fragrant, symphonic splendor.
Unfolding for my spiritual and sensual delight,
Reminding me again and again,
You're at the world's controls.
The day is new and bright
And all will eventually be right.

God's Word for You
"Have I not commanded you? Be strong and courageous. Do not be afraid; do not be discouraged, for the LORD your God will be with you wherever you go." Joshua 1:9

Nothing

Lord, help me not waste your gifts -
Take your money and hoard it.
I read the Scripture story told by You
And start to squirm when the master asks
How much did you make buying and selling
Using what I entrusted to you?
The man with ten mina made ten.
His reward authority over ten cities.
Another man with ten mina made five.
His reward was authority over five cites.

Another man with ten mina made none.
Because he feared the harshness of the nobleman.
The man who did nothing with his investment,
Had what he held back taken from him, and
Given to the man with the most fruit from his efforts.
All were judged by their actions.
As the questions were asked by the nobleman
Many watched him and his servants.
I wonder what they learned.
I know what I have learned.

The status of my account will be required.
Lord, may there be something of value in mine.

The Lily

I'd like to add moments to my age,
Enhancing my span of life.
Why? When heaven will be so grand.
Anyway my desire is futile, Lord.
I've learned I cannot snatch even a night.
Lord, when I'm over-anxious,
Troubled with care,
Help me remember the splendid lily.
Tranquil and carefree,
Every daily need supplied,
By a Father whose love never fails,
In every act of trust,
May I be like the lily.

New Season

Lord, I slip into morning wakefulness.
Thoughts climb into my consciousness
Waiting to be examined one by one.

I respond to this new day first with gratitude.
I have a mind and body that functions
And live in a world awaiting my engagement.
.
My life and that of my loved ones is earthbound,
Full of challenging situations,
 And brimming with excitement, too.

Lord, I love this pace of exquisite peace,
In this new season of life.
Accomplishing the tasks You've given.

While also enjoying tranquility,
A walk in the gardens,
A jaunt on the lake path.

You've equipped me for this new life's season.
Activity without frenzy.
Joy runs through all I do.

God's Word for You
*"I praise you because I am fearfully and wonderfully
made; Your works are wonderful, I know that full
well." Psalm 139:14*

The F's

Lord, I'm living in the F's again,
Frantic over my schedule,
Frazzled over demands,
Frizzled by stupid decisions,
Fretting over the future.

I grumble and sigh.
Wait! There's another «F."
This "F" is the one You've given, Lord:
Freedom in and through You.
I can be free from worry, hurry, guilt, perfection!

Freed from these bondages forever
Unless I choose to imprison myself.
How foolish that would be!
Relief floods over me.
Thank you, Lord!

God's Word for You
"Since, then, you have been raised with Christ, set your hearts on things above, where Christ is, seated at the right hand of God. Set your minds on things above, not on earthly things. Colossians 3:1-3

Witness

Be wary, you who speak lies in the dark,
But have heard truth in the light.
Fear not death of the body,
Fear only the horrors of hell.
Hear the many voices raised in witness.
Jesus is worthy of worship,
The son of Man is God of all.
Acknowledge Him now and forever,
Before the angels of God.
Join the army of witnesses,
Don't wait until it's too late.

Lord, I will speak Your name
And tell of Your deeds
Until the day
I see Your face.
I am a witness.

God's Word for You
"But our citizenship is in heaven. And we eagerly await a Savior from there, the Lord Jesus Christ."
Philippians 3:20

Stuck

Lord, my mind is stuck
In the oops and ouches.
The things I did,
The things I didn't.
The hurts I've given.
The hurts I've felt.
Lord, I want to get unstuck.

I run to Your Word
King David's oops'
Comfort me.
Paul's travail of ouches
Encourage me.
Job's relief and returned prosperity
Inspire me.

These men moved forward.
They were able to get unstuck
And became victors.
So can I!
Hope shoots through me.
My mind begins to be renewed.
Thank you, Lord!

God's Word for You
*"No, in all these things we are more than conquerors
through him who loved us." Romans 8:37*

Aglow

Holy Spirit,
The hour to speak is here.
I will not be anxious.
I need to talk in defense.
I haven't planned my words.
I rely upon Your promise.
Spirit, You'll tell me what to say.

Lord, my soul is aglow
And filled with peace.
I'm where I've longed to be.
I've searched and
You've guided.
My heart shouts with joy.
I've sought this place diligently.

There's nowhere I'd rather be,
Always I shall stay -
Today, tomorrow, for eternity,
In the very center of Your will,
In the palm of the Master's hand.
Speaking Your truth,
Acting on Your behalf.

God's Word for You
"Now may the God of peace... equip you with everything good for doing his will, and may He work in us what is pleasing to Him, through Jesus Christ." Hebrews 13: 20-21

Rejection

Religious law experts,
Hinderers of truth,
Enraged with You Jesus,
Plotted and watched.
But truth prevailed.
The key was the cross.
Jesus Christ crucified and risen!
Wisdom of God.
My Lord and my God.

Lord, I've also known rejection
When I've spoken about You.
You say a slight against me,
Is a slight against You.
Rejection of me,
Is rejection of You.

Lord, I can't stop it from happening,
But I will shake it off
And count it a privilege
To experience a small measure
Of the burden you carried for Me.

God's Word for You
"If the world hates you, keep in mind that it hated me first." John 15:18.

Morning

Lord, I love our early morning together,
This special time of prayer,
But now the commitments of the day
Call me away.
Great Jesus,
Incredible Holy Spirit,
Magnificent Father.
In every situation of this day,
Come with me,
Have Your way.
Permeate my words and actions
With Your Divine Presence
Minute by minute,
Word by word,
Act by act.

God's Word for You

"For we are God's handiwork, created in Christ Jesus to do good works, which God prepared in advance for us to do." Ephesians 2:10

Ignited

The fire of creativity burns within me
Ignited by you Lord,
Forming ideas,
Combining thoughts,
Creating new images.
I never feel closer to You Lord
Than when I'm engaged in creative work.
May my thoughts and writing be worthy,
Of my great God
You are the inexhaustible source of all ideas,
In whose image I am made.
Awesome God, I bow within my spirit,
Visible to You alone.
I lift my arms and
Long to advance Your name,
To use my gifts with strength
In all I do to honor You.

Lord, I understand this important truth.
My gifts are given to me by You
For Your glory.
To be used diligently by me,
For Your honor.
My abilities are not to be hoarded or flaunted
Because they're not of me, or for me,
They're to be used through You,
For You, with You.
Lord, help me keep this in mind!

"As each has received a gift, use it to serve one another, as good stewards of God's varied grace: whoever speaks, as one who speaks oracles of God; whoever serves, as one who serves by the strength that God supplies—in order that in everything God may be glorified through Jesus Christ." 1Peter 4:10-11

Heaven

Heaven like leaven?
What a startling thought!
Hid in flour,
It impacts all.
A kingdom that spreads and grows
With powerful impact.
Heaven like a grain of mustard seed
Turned tree-home for wild birds
Growing huge with solid roots?
I like these ideas,
But I wonder
How can the kingdom be within me?
I don't understand how, but I believe.

God's Word for You
"He [Jesus] told them another parable. 'The kingdom of heaven is like leaven that a woman took and hid in three measures of flour, till it was all leavened.'" Matthew 13:33

Forever

Possessions rust and rot
While greed screams for more.
Lord, I prefer inexhaustible treasure,
Free from decay, safe from thieves.
The kind of treasure it pleases You
To give -- the Kingdom of heaven--
While I walk the soil of earth
You give me such great joy.
My heart is totally content.
You are my true treasure,
On my journey through life.
And one day when my soul is called,
These things I once sought
Will mean little or nothing in forever.

Forever is a word I can't fully comprehend
The idea is too big for my brain, Lord.
Now and soon are hard enough for me to grasp.
Best I leave forever to You, Lord.
It's enough for me to know
Someday I'll be with You always,
And we'll be together in glory
But help me, please,
As I live through each moment now.

God's Word for You
"The world and its desires pass away, but whoever does the will of God lives forever." 2 John 2:17

News-bearer

What shall I do this day, Lord,
To bring to those I meet
Saving knowledge about You?
May I be sensitive
To the values others hold,
To personal needs that might draw them,
And know how best to share the news,
That never stops being good.

Lord, reach into my heart,
Pluck out any fear or hesitation.
May I speak Your words of truth
About salvation, the very greatest news
That others will ever hear.
Lord, I often lack intuition.
Accepting man's rationalizations,
In denial of the significant Word of God.
Make me wise and brave and bold!

God's Word for You
"Preach the word; be ready in season and out of season; reprove, rebuke, and exhort, with complete patience and teaching." 2 Timothy 4:2

Magnificent Moments

As God's presence and glory
Rested upon the Tabernacle,
Lord, I visualize its brightness and splendor.

My greatest honor,
My highest privilege,
Are the moments when Your glory rests upon me.

I am in awe at Your presence.
Thank You for each magnificent moment,
When I'm aware of Your presence and nothing else.

Lord I close my eyes,
You are there.
In all Your glory.

God's Word for You
*"Now the appearance of the glory of the Lord was like
a devouring fire on the top of the mountain in the sight
of the people of Israel." Exodus 24:17*

Commitment

Dearest Jews, might you listen now?
Remember the Midianites attacks against you,
When you hid in caves and strongholds
And foes brought poverty upon you?
Your enemies had their way,
You best plans were inadequate.
Until you cried out to God.

Enemies will continue to plague you.
Look up, the Living God waits.
At every stage of history His love is true
And fully committed
Desiring to bless you.
Call upon Him.
And watch God act on Your behalf.

In Him, through Him, with Him,
All life comes from Him.
All life exists through Him.
All life moves toward completion in Him,
He is our safety.
In Him we live and move
And have our being!

God's Word for You
"He returned to the camp of Israel and called out,
"Get up! The Lord has given the Midianite camp into
your hands." Judges 7:15

126

The Narrow Door

Lord, I want to get in,
I'm squeezing.
I must get through.
 Why is that door so narrow?

Don't close it yet.
I'm almost in,
A little tug, help me Lord,
Maybe a shove.

Be glorified, Lord,
In my efforts,
 Thoughts,
 Desires.

Be glorified also somehow
In my failures,
Insecurities
And lacks.

Upon Your name I call
Thank you, Lord,
For pulling me in.
I give you my all.

God's Word for You
*"Enter in by the narrow gate; for wide is the gate and
broad is the. way that leads to destruction, and many
are those who enter in by it." Matthew 7:13*

Asking

Lord, I ask in Your name
Then wait and watch.
I ask of You and You give
Over and over.

You've done all You promised,
More than I could have imagined.
In this You say the Father is exalted
Through my asking and Your giving.

Jesus, You in the Father.
Me in You, You in me.
Us in the Father.
All one in the Spirit .

How amazing.
I'm speechless and breathless.
Your blessings are incredible!
Mind-boggling.
"Ask, and it shall be given you;
Seek, and you shall find;
Knock, and it shall be opened unto you.
For every one who asks receives
And he that seeks finds,
And to him who knocks it shall be opened."

God's Word for You
*"Ask, and it shall be given you; seek, and you shall find;
knock and it will be opened unto you." Matthew 7:7*

Light - Shine

The light-shine in my heart
Comes from experiencing the light
Of the knowledge
Of the glory of God
From the face of Christ.
This light is the only brightness
That will shine forever -
Truly the light of the world.

This legacy of light
Is God's gift to me,
And to all with eyes to see,
Making the world
Better, brighter, stronger,
And everything in it
Radiant through Him –
The Creator of Light in the world.

God's Word for You
"I am the light of the world. Whoever follows me will never walk in darkness, but will have the light of life."
John 8:12

Signs of Need

I discern the looks of the sky and earth
And know when rain comes,
When a tornado approaches,
Or where a hurricane may strike,
But often fail to read signs of need all around.

Lord, You ask me to judge what is just,
Determine what is right.
Identify and abhor all evil,
Perceive approaching moral dangers
Use caution to avoid perishing eternally.

When You wish to work through me,
I want to be available to meet needs,
Not too pre-occupied with my own concerns.
Lord, may Your people be visible to me.
I want to reverence others as you do.

May I have a passion for Your people
A heart as responsive as Yours.
Lord, help me discern wisely
Between good and evil,
And the signs of need around me.

God's Word for You
*"As each has received a gift, use it to serve one
another, as good stewards of God's varied grace."*
1Peter 4:10

Enough

Lord, before I knew You,
I feared not being good enough,
Never being worthy,
To merit an eternity of heavenly joy.
How excited I was to learn
I didn't have to earn it.
Your conquest at Calvary,
Was enough for me.

But since, then Lord,
I've feared not doing enough
To prove worthy of Your great love,
How many souls can I help save for You?
How many lives can I help make right?

"Enough, You say, cease!"
You give me freedom, not frenzy
I mustn't exchange one bondage for another.

It's not by my doing that I most please You
But by quiet time spent with You,
By the holy life I live for You."

God's Word for You
"It is for freedom that Christ has set us free. Stand firm, then, and do not let yourselves be burdened again by a yoke of slavery." Galatians 5:1

My Best

Lord, I used to work to please myself
Or to meet the demands of others,
Now I work heartily from my soul,
Doing my very best for You,
Knowing in all things I serve You.
Someday my work will be made known,
Shown for what it is,
Revealed and tested with fire,
Examined for its character and worth.

Was it truly my best?
Only the work that survives this test
Will receive its reward.
For this you promise an inheritance
Greater than eye has ever seen.
What a reward!
Lord, You can be sure of this,
You'll have nothing
But my best from me.

God's Word for You
*"Whatever you do, work at it with all your heart, as
though working for the Lord, not for people."
Colossians 3:23*

Effect

Why is it wrong to sin Lord?
How does my wrongdoing hurt others?
Isn't sin all about me?
What does sin do?

"Sin causes distress and pain
For entire families.
And seeps into society.
Sin has huge consequences for others too."

Lord, You want everyone free of this stress
Including me.
Lord help me remember this.
Sin isn't only about me.

Keep me strong,
During my moments of temptation.
You promise to always provide a way out.
May I be quick to respond well.

God's Word for You
*"There hath no temptation taken you but such as is
common to man: but God is faithful, who will not
suffer you to be tempted above that ye are able; but
will with the temptation also make a way to escape,
that ye may be able to bear it." 1 Corinthians 10:1*

Cleansing

Lord, cleanse me –
My mind,
My heart, and
My mouth.
Lord, messy specks of verbal dirt,
Mental balls of prideful dust,
The murky film of a selfish heart
Seem to appear from nowhere.

Lord, how I need You,
Holiness eludes me.
Your continual cleansing is needed.
Wipe me down, rinse me out, purify me,
I dedicate myself to You,
My mind,
My mouth,
My heart.

God's Word for You
"Have mercy upon me, O God, according to thy lovingkindness: according unto the multitude of thy tender mercies not out my transgressions. Wash me thoroughly from mine iniquity, and cleanse me from my sin. For I acknowledge my transgressions: and my sin is ever before me." Psalm 51:1-3

Hands Up

"I lift my hands as an evening sacrifice,"
Said King David in Psalm 141.
Accept my upraised hands also Lord as offering.

Hands up, emotion visible,
Heart swelling, emotion invisible,
Sign of the connection between God and David.

Sign of the connection between God and me.
My hands reach toward You Lord,
Through this expression of honor.

Others may stare perplexed,
A few may disdain my display,
I care not who sees or what they say.

Hands up, with my eyes closed
The air between us becomes electrified.
I am aware of Your presence – above all else.

God's Word for You
"I call to you, Lord, come quickly to me; hear me when I call to you. May my prayer be set before you like incense; may the lifting up of my hands be like the evening sacrifice." Psalm 141:1-2

Re-Joy

Lord, the Word says
Joy is an order,

Then re-joy.
Find it again,

And then again.
And again.

Create it with a smile,
As you bless those you pass.

Use it to sweeten your day
Keep a laugh-in-waiting,

Satan likes to use the blues
In place of the joy You desire for me

Circumstances are temporal,
Joy is eternal.

Joy and laughter
Are my heritage.

I will re-joy
In glorious joy today.

God's Word for You
*"There, in the presence of the Lord your God, you and
your families shall eat and shall rejoice in everything
you have put your hand to, because the Lord your God
has blessed you." Deuteronomy 12:7*

Faith

Holy fire of faith,
Burn brightly in me
Be a persistent fire
A warming fire,
A Holy Spirit tongue-licking fire.
That I can walk through safely

Holy fire of faith
Consume my impurities
Set me ablaze
With fire that never ceases.
For I long to please Jesus,
The One Who set me aflame.

God's Word for You
"Very truly I tell you, whoever believes in me will do the works I have been doing, and they will do even greater things than these, because I am going to the Father." John 14:12

First Church

Lord, before you hosted the 5000,
At Your impromptu outdoor dinner,
You commanded them to recline in groups
On the green grass.
They listened and followed orders
Throwing themselves down in ranks
At your request
Of hundreds and fifties
Looking like orderly beds of herbs in garden plots.
Lord, why did you want them in groups?
Were You teaching them the value even then
Of experiencing church community?
That meal – this first communion,
A feasting on physical bread of life
Was a hint of the greater bread to come.
Best received in unity with others.
They were eager to receive the life You provided
Lord, may your menus of loaves and fishes
Help me remember
The importance of attending church,
Being in the presence of other believers,
In orderly groups
Is right for my body and my soul.

God's Word for You
"Do you still not understand? Don't you remember the five loaves for the five thousand, and how many basketfuls you gathered?" Matthew 16:9

The Course

The lessons have been given,
The whole course taught.
Lord You said, "I've made known
Everything I heard from My Father.
Now the Holy Spirit will speak into your heart."
The result is up to me.

What kind of student will I be?
One who absorbs and remembers
Or one who ignores and forgets?
Your grade is not like a school letter,
Nothing less than heaven or hell.
May I be a diligent learner!

Lord, You're an amazing teacher.
I'm honored to learn from You.

God's Word for You
*"...because He [Jesus] taught as one who had authority,
and not as their teachers of the law." Matthew 7:29*

Fruit

Lord, You've planted me,
And nurtured me,
To be Your luscious fruit,
Yes, first a seed, then a flower,
And then more.

Planted for a purpose,
That whatever I do for others
Can be empowered by You.
That whatever I ask in the Father's name,
In accord with His will, He will give.

Five words sum up life's meaning:
Know, love and serve God!
Loving comes after knowing.
Loving comes before serving,
Serving must be humble, free, passionate.

This is the purpose for all human beings
And the reward for responsive souls.
These words describe the greatest of goals,
The grandest of plans and the superb result -
An energized, transformed, holy life.

God's Word for You
*"You did not choose me, but I chose you and
appointed you so that you might go and bear fruit —
fruit that will last." John 15:16*

Path

Lord, I desire to walk in Your will,
Only show me the path.
Now, Lord, if you please.
I'm at a crossroads again.
There are many forks I could follow.
Which shall I choose?
What is best for me?

Lord, I'm longing to know,
Eager to serve.
Send my light where human light is dim
Or where it's already begun to glow.
Send me where salt is required.
Shake me out generously,
Guide me where I should go.

God's Word for You
"The steps of a good man are ordered by the Lord."
Psalm 37:23

Hatred

Lord, Your Word is clear.
The world's hatred is natural.
I can expect it, command it!
Detested by the world?
Hated because I'm Yours?
This makes me glad!
Lord, Your Word suggests:
Shun affection from truth-distorters.
Fear being loved as the world's own,
I'm no longer one with them.
I've been rescued from their grasp,

Lord, faithfully You remind me,
In words that speak to my heart:
Fear not the world.
I'm totally loved,
And Your beloved treasure."

God's Word for You
"How priceless is your unfailing love, O God! People take refuge in the shadow of your wings." Psalm 36:7

Yes, I Am

God, You say about Yourself:
"Yes, I am with you on the stony paths.
Yes, I am on your smooth roads.
Yes, I am in the squawk of your noisy problem.
Yes, I am in the depth of your shadows.
Yes, I am in your total darkness.
Yes, I am in your breaths of delight.
Yes, I am in the sobs of your sorrow.
Yes, I know where You walk now.
Yes, My unseen arms encircle you always,
Yes, my plan for you is great and good.
Yes, I care, and know all.
Yes, you can trust me in everything.
Yes, unending hope is my gift to you.
Yes, I am your God."

God's Word for You
"May the God of hope fill you with all joy and peace as you trust in him, so that you may overflow with hope by the power of the Holy Spirit." Romans 15:13

Holy Spirit

Holy Spirit, wondrous breath of God,
You charged the earth
With an explosion of Your presence
When You appeared after Jesus' Resurrection
To the frightened few who loved You.

Holy Spirit, wondrous gift of God,
You've imploded into my life!
And transformed everything.
Heaven is no longer far off.
The Kingdom is here.

Your fruit, Your gifts,
Mine upon our acceptance,
Empowered by my commitment,
Fill me with spirit-life,
Real, relevant, ever-present.

You enable me to minister to others,
Meet apparent needs around me,
Actually impact the universe
Through Your spiritual power,
Awesome Holy Spirit.

God's Word for You
"But you shall receive power when the Holy Spirit has come upon you; and you shall be witnesses to Me in Jerusalem, and in all Judea and Samaria, and to the end of the earth." Acts 1:8

Grace

Grace is simple, invisible, powerful.
Grace is free, valuable and available!
Grace empowers us to be:
Responsible,
Articulate,
Kind,
Persevering,
Confident.
Grace and truth must be defended
From marauders prowling about.
Knowledge sharpens my soul.
Study prepares me
For the onslaught that surely comes.
Holy Spirit, equip me for this battle.

God's Word for You
"When he [Peter] arrived and saw what the grace of God had done, he was glad and encouraged them all to remain true to the Lord with all their hearts. Acts 11:23

Unfought Battles

How many spiritual battles have never been fought?
How many modern day Gideons lacked courage?
What Daniels didn't remain consistent in faith?
How many 21st century warriors chose the way of non-involvement?

How many faltered before achieving victory because prayer cover stopped?
What Davids were too fearful to fight their Goliaths?
How many rebuilders like Nehemiah didn't seek
God's plan first?
Which Esthers have said, "I've not been chosen for this?"

Lord, we've been given all we need to win Your battles,
When we use the equipment You supply,
But we must be courageous and willing to fight.
Lord, may I be so!

God's Word for You
"When you go out to battle against enemies, and see horses, and chariots, and a people more than you, be not afraid of them: for the Lord thy God is with you, Who brought you up out of the land of Egypt."
Deuteronomy 20:1

Mountain

Lord, You tell me speak to a mountain
And it will move.
Often, I must first move the mountain
Of my own inertia.
Which can build within me overnight
 Massively impeding my efforts,
Creating within me self-absorption
Blocking my eagerness to reach out,
And laziness that interferes
With using my gifts to nurture Your kingdom.

Mountain, move out of my way!
I must advance as my Master directs.
In His name, I give the command.

God's Word for You
"And Jesus said to them [the Apostles], 'Because you have so little faith. Truly I tell you, if you have faith as small as a mustard seed, you can say to this mountain, 'Move from here to there,' and it will move. Nothing will be impossible for you.'" Matthew 17:20.

Losers

The stories of winners who became losers abound.
Uzziah became proud.
A loser!
Saul became jealous.
A loser!
Solomon became a wife-pleaser.
A loser!
Hezekiah became a show-off.
A loser!
Judas became a traitor.
A loser!
Lord, by the power of Your Spirit,
I want to be a winner!

God's Word for You
"But when he [Uzziah the King] was strong, his heart was lifted up to his destruction: for he transgressed against the Lord his God, and went into the temple of the Lord to burn incense upon the altar of incense."
2 Chronicles 26:16-18

Theudas

Theudas, it's said that you desired to be great,
And persuaded 400 men to trust in you.
They followed closely for a time.
But because of your hypocrisy,
Your movement came to nothing.
You were killed.
Your followers went their separate ways.

When Jesus, Son of God, died
His Spirit empowered many.
They boldly proclaimed with holiness and truth
The reality of His great, good news.
And when their mouths were closed in sacrificial death,
Their souls still shouted "Hosanna,
God walks among us and lives still."

This is the difference between pretense and actuality-
Lasting greatness flows from inherent goodness.

God's Word for You
"Some time ago Theudas appeared, claiming to be somebody, and about four hundred men rallied to him. He was killed, all his followers were dispersed, and it all came to nothing." Acts 5:36

Remember – Forget

Lord, the Israelites Your chosen people,
Have quite a record of
Remember – forget.
How could they be so foolish!
One day they honor You,
Remembering Your great kindness and many
deliverances,
Then soon forget Your presence and past provisions.
Remember – forget.
Lord, I too must recall
The victories You've won for me.
You tell me to recount Your deeds often.
Lord, may I always remember and
Never forget for one moment.
Mistaken thoughts are easy.
Grumbling about my lot.
Many is too few,
Much is never enough.
If a little is good,
A lot is better,
If I want, I can.
If they have… I should have.
Mistaken thoughts indeed!

Lord, I think I get it now.
Remembering is important!
Trust is essential!
It's all about You and me.

We're a past and future team.
You're the leader
And I'm the follower.
If I keep this in mind,
We're unstoppable.
Victory is certain.

God's Word for You
"Remember what God has done for you. Let His grace and mercy comfort you, and remind you of His unfailing love." Psalm 143:4

Heavenly Residence

Lord, fire flames high in my imagination.
Reality crumbles around me.
The depth of dangerous waters leaves me gasping.
Then with the tiniest of breaths
My praise whispers forth.
You're always worthy of my alleluia.

The chorus of nature breaks into deafening praise.
Sky, earth, air clap in unison.
The God of then is the God of now.
My knees collapse in worship.
My body is fully here and completely aware,
While my soul takes up heavenly residence.

This is prayer!
This is praise!

God's Word for You
*"Then they cried to the Lord in their trouble, and he
delivered them from their distress. He made the storm
be still, and the waves of the sea were hushed."*
Psalm 107:28-29

Dancing With Angels

Lord, it's me,
Dancing with the angels.
Watch me dip and spin.
All because of this great joy within.
Lord, my heart no longer touches earth,
Though my body stays in place.
I'm in the Kingdom fully come,
Your servant, beloved, holy one.
I'm told eternity shows on my face,
Yet I'm only reflecting Your grace.
Lord, it's the dance divine,
Already forever mine.
Lord of giggles,
Lord of laughs,
Lord of roars.
Fun, my wondrous Lord,
Is knowing, loving and serving You!

God's Word for You
"And I commend joy, for man has no good thing under the sun but to eat and drink and be joyful, for this will go with him in his toil through the days of his life that God has given him under the sun." Ecclesiastes 8:15

Forgiving

Oh my God,
I'm in awe over You.
Mocked, beaten, stabbed,
Rejected, cursed, humiliated.
Such sacrifice is beyond imagination
After Your acts of kindness-
Foot-washing, serving and loving Your tormentors.

Jesus, You remained silent before Your accusers.
Yet, how I rush to defend myself from the slightest
criticism.
Silence requires self-denial and ends self-
righteousness.
Lord, may I be capable of keeping my mouth closed,
When silence may better speak Your truth.

What fools would hurt You like this?
Perhaps a fool like me who
Neglects reading Your biblical letters,
Ignores the intimate communication in Your Word
And often forgets I'm in Your presence every moment.
Lord, You forgave them, please forgive me.

God's Word for You
*"And Jesus said, 'Father, forgive them, for they know
not what they do.'" Luke 23:34*

God's Numbers

Lord, You certainly use small numbers well.
Gideon's 300 men were victorious against 120,000.
In the book of Joshua, one man put 1000 to flight.
A few loaves and fishes fed 5000,
All You require, Lord, is reverent fear of You,
And service to You in sincerity and in truth,
To release Your mighty hand.
You reveal Your control over natural law.
Warriors fall, food appears, the world changes,
All upon Your divine command.
Lord, these lessons from numbers amaze me!
And comfort me in our world today.

God's Word for You
*"One man of you shall chase a thousand, for the Lord
your God is He who fights for you, as He promised you."
Joshua 23:10 NKJV*

The Grand Pretend

Having and doing,
Moving and grooving.
Life on the surface.
The grand pretend,
Smiles and laughter,
Concealing confusion well.
Is this truly all?
Shouldn't there be something else
In our splendid drama of life?
Every now and then,
We catch a glimpse.
Somehow our heart knows,
There is much more.
Someone knows truth,
The One who made meaning itself,
Shows life beneath and beyond,
And teaches what real living is.

Lord, You are my truth speaker,
You are the truth teacher,
You are the truth source.

I surrender ignorance,
I forsake mental inadequacy,
I seek Your gifts, I crave Your fruit.

Yours is the truth fountain within my soul,
May it flow continuously.
That I may spout godly wisdom.

Incomparable

You, Lord, are incredulous.
That You should love me!
All that You do for me!
The miracles You work!
Truly incomprehensible!
Utterly incomparable!

Lord, the thrill of Your Presence,
The power of Your truth,
The richness You bring to my life!
How could anyone deny You?

Immersed in Your creation,
You soothe my soul.
You move my mind from dilemmas to dreams,
From petty nothings to precise somethings,
From problems to possibilities.

God's Word for You
"In order that in the coming ages he might show the incomparable riches of his grace, expressed in his kindness to us in Christ Jesus." Ephesians 2:7

Controversy

Lord, what controversy you stirred.
People hotly disputed that you were a good man
Many thought you deceived and misled the masses.

The mystery of your past baffled the Jews.
Where had you acquired such knowledge of Scripture?
You had never studied with a rabbi.

You said all can know truth
Lord it had to be confusing for people
The Jews hadn't expected a gentle Messiah.

And you were from Bethlehem, then Nazareth
Saying You hadn't come of Your own accord,
But because God the Father sent you.

I can only imagine the uproar that followed
And the excitement in the hearts of those who finally
believed!
Because I know the thrill in my own heart!

God's Word for You
*"Jesus answered, 'My teaching is not my own. It comes
from the one who sent me. Anyone who chooses to do
the will of God will find out whether My teaching comes
from God or whether I speak on My own."*
John 7:16-17

Power of Faith

Faith, don't flee
In my moment of need.
Stay with me.
My heart must be lifted
To an awareness of eternity,
Even while this present reality
Consumes my being.
Only faith can transcend the gap
Between my fear and my hope.
Yet must I believe!
Yet will I believe!

Lord, I need You.
I love You.
I desire You.

I praise You.
I thank You.
I treasure You.
Always,
Forever,
As long as ever.

Lord, I know You are:
Good,
Glorious,
Gracious.

Lord, Your Word is
High,
Holy,
Hope-filled.
How happy my life,
Lived with faith in You.

God's Word for You

"For by grace you have been saved through faith. And this is not your own doing; it is the gift of God."
Ephesians 2:8

Humility

Humility lost,
Humility regained:
Eve in the Garden forgot humility
Her desire for knowledge led to the fall.

Humility was absent in Saul.
He desired to be the greatest
So the popular warrior David he tried to kill,
Then God required Saul's life.

Jesus lived humility to perfection,
Humility led to His cross.
Ultimately humility drew the highest honor,
From the Creator of Personhood.

Why does pride ever pull upon my heart?
If ultimate glory lies in contentment,
Willingness to kneel before the Lord.
Oh for the strength and wisdom to be free of me.

God's Word for You
*"Do nothing out of selfish ambition or vain conceit.
Rather, in humility value others above yourselves."
Philippians 2:3*

Disciples

Lord, Your command is clear
Go make disciples.
Whoever knew making disciples would be this much fun?

You've made such interesting people
What a privilege to touch their hearts
With Your truth.

I watch their souls come alive
And see their minds expand with truth.
They become Word hungry and are Spirit-fed.

Lord, You made me a warrior.
A warrior of the Word,
In the Word, for the Word.

All because You commanded:
"Go make disciples…"
Thanks, for giving me a few.

My weapon is sharp with power.
Help me wield my sword with accuracy.
That Your truth may prevail.

God's Word for You
"Therefore go and make disciples of all nations, baptizing them in the name of the Father and of the Son and of the Holy Spirit, and teaching them to obey everything I have commanded you." Matthew 28:19-20

Divine Training

Why is serving where we're observed,
Easier than serving where we're unseen?

Why is giving where it's noticed
Easier than giving where it's not?

Why is hurting easier than the alternative?
Lovingly confronting and resolving pain.

Why is hating easier than forgiving?
Getting better than giving generously.

Destroying can be done inattentively.
Building up takes thought.

Lord, Your training program is specific:
Fear no person.
Praise before receiving blessings.
Choose always to trust.
Wait with hope. Dread no disaster.
Accept reality. Rejoice with abandon.
Forgive without resentment.
Pray about everything.
Anticipate heaven's reward.
Simple, concise, clear requirements
For the child of God,
The soldier of Christ,
A vessel of the Holy Spirit.
May I serve You well.
May we all.

Symbols

Lord, you often used symbols to speak about Yourself.
You said You are:
Like a Gate – I can walk through.
Like a Door – I can open.
Bread of Life – I can taste and be nourished.
Like Water – I can drink and be sustained.
Like a Shepherd – I can be guided and protected by You.
All this and more You are.
These symbols speak of divine reality.

Knowing

I know You better Lord,
Through every answered prayer from yesterday.
I know You better, Lord,
From every glimpse of Your creation today.
And I'll know You yet better tomorrow,
Lord, our adventure ever unfolds!

Lord, I know little about others' heart history with you.
I only know holy moments exist between you and me.
And I savor every second with You.
You're as close as Your name.
Lord, I have only to think of You
And I want to fall on my knees.

God's Word for You
"This is what the LORD says: 'Let not the wise boast of their wisdom or the strong boast of their strength or the rich boast of their riches, but let the one who boasts boast about this: that they have the understanding to know me, that I am the LORD, who exercises kindness, justice and righteousness on earth, for in these I delight,' declares the LORD."
Jeremiah 9: 23-24

Honor

Lord, religious leaders attacked You,
Said You were evil –
You, the God of all good,
Under the power of a demonic spirit?
How ridiculous a claim!
You answered, "I don't seek honor for myself.
I desire reverence for my Father."
And for this they hated You.

Your lesson is clear
I must not seek honor for My own glory.
The opinion of people is irrelevant.
You modeled the humility I must have
And the single-minded focus on Our Father.

Lord, I'd like to say I'm ready for anything.
But serving beyond my comfort zone scares me.
I need Your grace, Your power, Lord.
Make me a fearless supernatural server,
Equipped with Spirit energy.
I can't do it by myself.

God's Word for You
"I am not possessed by a demon," said Jesus, "but I honor my Father and you dishonor me. I am not seeking glory for myself." John 8:48-49

Breathe

Breathe deep within me, Holy Spirit.
Draw all impurities from me.
Filter them through Your fiery goodness
That I may exhale purity.

May Your breath fill my being
Then permeate the atmosphere.
But not my breath, Holy Spirit,
Yours alone holds power to transform.

My life quest is simple:
Forsaking fame or wealth,
Becoming the me God made me to be.
Nothing less, nothing more.

My lifelong goal is solely
Serving forever the God I adore.
This is my ultimate reality,
With the Spirit's help, My highest joy!

God's Word for You
"But you will receive power when the Holy Spirit comes on you; and you will be my witnesses in Jerusalem, and in all Judea and Samaria, and to the ends of the earth." Acts 1:8

Fragments

Lord, 5000 were fed, leaving fragments of bread and fish.
You sent Your disciples to gather 12 baskets of leftovers,
Lest the broken pieces that remained be wasted.

Lord, in the past I have felt like a broken piece,
I visualize You sending disciples to gather me in,
Lest I be wasted or lost.

Fragments, broken pieces matter to You, Lord.
Use me now to gather up others
That none may be wasted.

God's Word for You
"Jesus then took the loaves, gave thanks, and distributed to those who were seated as much as they wanted. He did the same with the fish... gather the pieces that are left over. Let nothing be wasted." John 6:23

Mary Model

Mary, many call you gentle,
And I'm sure you were,
But few speak of your strength.

When your life became confusing
You trusted an angelic messenger,
Committing your body and soul to magnify God.

You endured the travail of your baby's birthing day,
And hurriedly fled under cover of darkness
To guard your precious miracle child.

Years of sweet silence follow,
Nurturing the child born to nurture others.
Loving and training this Son of Man and God.

You endured Jesus' horrid death on a cross
And the evenings of sorrow in the Upper Room
Until you beheld your Son again.

Your son honored You with his dying breath,
And provided for your continual care,
Forever grateful to You for mothering Him.

Mary, may I remember that your strength -
Tough and gentle –
Is God's loving legacy to me as well.

"When Jesus therefore saw His mother, and the disciple whom He loved standing by, He said to His mother, 'Woman, behold your son!' Then He said to the disciple, 'Behold your mother!' And from that hour that disciple took her to his own home." John 19:26-27

Wisdom of God

The wisdom of God
Was delivered according to plan,
Decreed for my glorification.
Designed to remove my ignorance,
Compensate for my unworthiness,
And lift me straight into paradise!
Incomprehensible, superb!

Lord, awards and accolades give only momentary joy.
You said don't toil in order to produce what rots and rusts,
Create instead what's lasting and unchanging.
Impacting lives for Christ
Creates meaning and purpose for a lifetime.
The perfect plan for man,
The wisdom of God.

God's Word for You
"For the Lord gives wisdom; From His mouth [come] knowledge and understanding." Proverbs 2:6

Women

Lord, You always know what women need.
You knew Martha needed rest and reminded her what was best.
You reminded the woman at the well that she needed true love
Greater than five husbands could provide.

You helped Mary Magdalene see her soul had the capacity to glow
And she experienced the joy of being clean again.
You knew Lydia loved to serve and
Enabled her to generously give to those in need.

You used Deborah to judge with wisdom.
You took Mary from her household to parent Your Son,
Her saintliness made her worthy
And she became a female model of holiness.

I treasure my womanhood.
You have selected my sex for me.
You gifted women to do amazing things.
Examples of brave women abound in Scripture.

You guide each woman toward her personal fulfillment.
Your desire is that all women be blessed.
You've made it clear in the examples set before me
I can depend on You to guide me to my very best.

Irresistible

Irresistible Lord,
That's what You are to me.
I long to make You irresistible to others.
How can I make You, my invisible Lord, visible?

Lord, Your life story is not simply an ancient text,
But current and relevant.
You send Your Spirit to work in lives receptive to You.
Become visible, Lord, through me!

Lord, help me inspire others to discover You
Who will be faithful and honor You.
I long for my family, my friends, all I meet
To know the joy of Your love, the power of Your influence.
And find You irresistible, too!

God's Word for You
"But let all who take refuge in You rejoice; let them sing joyful praises forever. Spread Your protection over them, that all who love Your name may be filled with joy." Psalm 5:11

Battle Cry

Lord, it's comforting to know
You do what is good in Your sight-
Although, not necessarily in mine.

I see only a small piece of reality -
My tiny time of present, limited glimpses of the past
And none of the future with certainty.

Lord, it's easy to allow myself to feel cast down,
To become disquieted within my inner self.
Until, Lord, I remember this.

Then my trust grows strong within me
And peace and joy explode again.
Your plan always results in my best.

Joab prayed before battle:
"Be of good courage and may the Lord
Do what is good in His sight."

Whatever experiences I face in life,
This, too, shall be my battle cry.
"Lord, I shall do what is good in Your sight."

God's Word for You
"The Lord will do what is good in His sight."
1 Chronicles 19:13

That You Would

Jesus, it's mind-boggling that You came,
Graciously, purposely entered earth.
You knew the future, but still You came.

You found me and I embraced You.
I've come to know the power of Your name,
And the intensity of Your love.

I'm so very glad!
Since I've discovered this truth,
Life has never been the same!

Lord, I'm amazed.
I will shout it,
Dance about it!

That You would,
That You could,
Love me like You do!

God's Word for You
"And may you have the power to understand, as all God's people should, how wide, how long, how high, and how deep His love is. May you experience the love of Christ, though it is too great to understand fully."
Ephesians 3:18

Quiet Christian

Lord, sometimes I'm too quiet a Christian.
I haven't begun to serve You with total effort,
Complete humility and shed tears.
No death plots like Paul's face me
 For speaking out about You.

I'm not constantly risking prison or hardships.
No, I am too often silent
Or I send Your truth forth in tiny pieces,
Making my own decisions about what and whether
Someone's ready to hear.

I long to be Spirit-coached
Always responsive to Your leading.
Concerned about defending You
More than about offending a listener.
Fearless and brave is my desire.

May I be bold like Paul.
He never hesitated to preach something helpful to
another,
Proclaiming the whole will of God.
Guide my mouth, Lord,
That I may speak Your truth into this world.

God's Word for You
*"He [Paul] proclaimed the kingdom of God and
taught about the Lord Jesus Christ—with all boldness
and without hindrance!" Acts 28:31*

Revelation Numbers

Lord, how varied are the numbers in Revelation:
1 throne of heaven encircled by an emerald rainbow
where all began,
4 living creatures - lion, ox, man and flying eagle
surround it,
6 wings on each creature covered with eyes all around.
7-fold Spirit of God!
7 lamps blazing before the throne,
24 elders in white with golden crowns,
24 golden bowls filled with saints' prayers,
24 thrones upon which they sat.
10,000 x 10,0000 angels before the throne.
1 scroll sealed with 7 seals,
1 Lion of Judah to open the scroll,
Rumblings and peals of thunder,
Numerous flashes of lightning.
Numbers of power!
Scene of praise!
All mankind one day shall bow.
My heart responds with boundless awe.

God's Word for You
*"This calls for wisdom. Let the person who has insight
calculate the number of the beast, for it is the number
of a man. That number is 666." Revelation 13:18*

Riddles

Lord, You often spoke in riddles,
Made outrageous demands,
And gave mysterious commands.
Why such hype and hoopla?
Were riddles to make people think,
Mysteries to make us wonder?

You equipped us well with power to decipher truth
And the ability for unraveling puzzles,
As well as a great capacity for faith.
We're able to acquire knowledge,
As we consider facts before us,
And sincerely search for understanding.

Lord, when I probe what You ask of us,
And study the consequences of following Your plan,
The riddles unravel into solid reason,
Your demands become pure safety,
Your commands display incredible love
Riddles and mystery fade away.

God's Word for You
*"Son of man, propound a riddle and speak a parable
to the house of Israel, saying, 'Thus says the Lord
God." Ezekiel 17:2-3*

Celebrations

Lord, I'd like a celebration day for creation.
The day Your brilliance first shone into our world.
From one creative act, the simple command
"Let there be light,"
Brightness cycled into time,
differentiating days and seasons,
Breaking forever the strength of darkness.

How about a somber celebration for the cross,
As prelude to the Easter Resurrection day,
Potent renewal of life for humankind,
This bewildering, incredible true story
Of one death birthing multiple eternal lives.

I'd like an Upper Room gala celebration of the
empowerment of man?
By divine decree universal access to the fullness of
God was promised
As the Holy Spirit took up permanent residence in time,
Cycling brightly through generations, never to be
quenched.

The celebration of Christmas commemorates
The day of new beginning for the relationship of God
with man,
The night even earth's brightness became extraordinary
As Christ in flesh entered the world He'd made,
Exciting first shepherds and kings, then all mankind.

Lord, humbly I celebrate Your extraordinary reality.
I have walked in Your warmth, I have experienced
Your comfort,
You have ignited my life and fired my soul.
How worthy You are of all these commemorations,
Because of You my celebrations shall never cease.

God's Word for You
"Now this day will be a memorial to you, and you shall celebrate it as a feast to the Lord; throughout your generations you are to celebrate it as a permanent ordinance." Exodus 12:14

Heaven's Pages

The heavenly host observe carefully,
As God supernaturalizes human choices and actions.
The ever-watchful angels
Joyfully record each new life in heaven's pages.

Divinity resides within us,
When we demonstrate Our Father's love.
Empty souls and needy bodies discover
That God alone can fill every need.

And heaven's pages multiply.

God's Word for You
"He who overcomes will thus be clothed in white garments; and I will not erase his name from the book of life, and I will confess his name before My Father and before His angels." Revelation 3:5

Adventure

As I forge into this new day
May I not fret a second away.
I choose to stride with purpose
Into its unfolding adventure,
Secure in the affection of family and friends,
Enriched by laughter and love,
Guarded by the host of heaven,
I surrender complacency and comfort
To serve my Master worthy of my best.
My God,
My life,
My all.
Lord, You give me such daily power!
Power in what I say or don't say
To affect people and events now and in the future.
My glance can show displeasure that disheartens
Or affirmation that encourages.
Lord, I want to use my power well,
I can build or destroy so easily.
May I be mindful of my responsibility
And serve You well Master, worthy of my best.

God's Word for You
"Whatever you do, work heartily, as for the Lord and not for men, knowing that from the Lord you will receive the inheritance as your reward. You are serving the Lord Christ." Colossians 3:23-24

Secrets

Important secrets have been revealed:
We know Who made us.
We know why we were made.
We can know where we're going.
We know the secret to receiving is in giving.
And the way to success is servanthood.
Other things may be a secret,
But these things we know.
Precious truths are ours:

Nothing and no one compares to You, Lord,
Nothing and no one takes priority over You, Lord,
Nothing must come before my focus on You, Lord.
No service of love is more valuable than loving You.
The events of my life may be challenging or dull,
Momentarily exciting and fun, but
Always they are temporary and insignificant
When placed in heavenly perspective, Lord!
Important secrets all can know.

God's Word for You
*"For there is nothing hidden that will not be disclosed,
and nothing concealed that will not be known or
brought out into the open." Luke 8:17*

Judges

Lord, me a judge? Yes, You say.
You made Your people judges,
Not of salvation, but of behavior
To motivate others to live well for You.

Yet You require judging in a particular way:
Do not decide at a glance,
Which would be superficial.

Judge with kindness and fairness,
Judge with honesty and clarity,
Judge with thoughtfulness.

Judge between godly teaching and wayward teaching.
Judge whether responses are to God's authority or man's.
Judge who needs encouragement or chastisement.

Judge only those seeking to do God's will.
Sinners don't know any better,
God's people are expected to.

Lord, You offer those judges the gift of illumination,
Who sincerely see Your will.
Lord, may all my judgments be true.
May I build up those I humbly judge for You.

God's Word for You
"Stop judging by mere appearances, but instead judge correctly." John 7: 24

Sin Shock

Me a sinner?
Me in need of repentance?
Am I really that bad?
The thought shocks me until I recall:
The times I don't care that my words pierce like arrows,
While I damage or destroy another's self-esteem,
The moments my acts are motivated by self-
advancement,
As I greedily grab for what I perceive to be best.

Yet, Lord, You love me even in this sinful state
And willingly became my Lord,
You cleanse and change me,
Showing me the ugly motives behind my deeds,
Teaching me that less can mean more
And last can become first.
Lord, I admit to being a well-seasoned sinner,
And joyfully one You're turning into a saint!

God's Word for You
*"You know that he [Jesus] appeared in order to take
away sins, and in him there is no sin. No one who
abides in him keeps on sinning; no one who keeps on
sinning has either seen him or known him."*
1John 3:5-6

Grace

Grace is
Incredible favor,
Loving kindness,
Forgiving mercy.

Grace is
 My inheritance,
My legacy,
My great gift.

Grace is
Given freely,
Without limitation,
By my gracious God.

God's Word for You
"Yet God, in his grace, freely makes us right in his sight. He did this through Christ Jesus when he freed us from the penalty for our sins." Romans 3:24

Glad

Lord, I'm glad You understand
That I'm afraid sometimes,
Even when I shouldn't be.

You didn't mind Nicodemus visiting at night out of fear
Or Gideon sacrificing the bull at night,
Lest the men of the city and his father's household know.

My courage is built slowly by experiences with Your grace.
Until my courage gets rooted firmly in place,
Thanks for being patient with me.

Special souls are in the white robe club,
Brave martyrs, slain for their testimony of the word of God.
They reside in heaven under the altar of Our Sovereign Lord.
And wait patiently for the Lord to judge their murderers,
When their number is complete.

Lord, if I should be invited into this select group,
I long to speak of Your name and deeds with integrity.
May my testimony be strong and true,
That I shall join this select group worthily
And well deserve my white robe.

God's Word for You
"Then they were each given a white robe and told to rest a little longer, until the number of their fellow servants and their brothers should be complete, who were to be killed as they themselves had been." Revelation 6:11

Singing Mountains

"Shout aloud oh earth beneath,
Burst into song you mountains,
You forests and all your trees.
Sing for joy oh heavens."

Lord, I long to hear these sounds that form
The music of Your creation -
The symphony of Your world in praise
All orchestrated by You.

Triumphant sounds permeate the planets,
Like when you rejoiced and rebuilt the nation of Israel,
Lord, like when you restore straying children.
I can imagine the sounds when You daily replenish
me!

God's Word for You
*"Sing for joy, you heavens, for the Lord has done this;
shout aloud, you earth beneath. Burst into song, you
mountains, you forests and all your trees..."*
Isaiah 44:23

The Unknowns

Unknowns among us have done great things,
Simple, but important, to God
And treasured by Him.

One such man, unknown to many, is Shapan,
A court secretary who read aloud a rediscovered scroll.
Other unknown men, Jahath and Obadiah, labored faithfully.

How often laborers, clerks, assistants remain unnamed,
Yet extraordinary spiritual events would not occur without them.
And their names are recorded in God's Book of Life.

The world honors celebrity.
Lord, You honor simplicity and humility.
And recognize and reward the unknowns among us.

God's Word for You
"The workers labored faithfully. Over them to direct them were Jahath and Obadiah, Levites descended from Merari, and Zechariah and Meshullam, descended from Kohath. The Levites... had charge of the laborers and supervised all the workers from job to job."
2 Chronicles 34:13

Joy and Grace

Salt and pepper,
Joy and grace,
Both are necessary ingredients
To season a life.

Joy in trials?
Yes, even then,
God's grace at work.
Joy in all.

Joy in suffering?
Yes, even then,
God's grace at work,
Joy in all.

Joy in waiting?
Yes, even then
God's grace at work,
Joy in all.

God's Word for You

"Count it all joy, my brothers, when you meet trials of various kinds, for you know that the testing of your faith produces steadfastness." James 1:2

Hupomone and Makrothumia

Where is my pleasant, orderly life?
This is not how my life was supposed to look.
How did these terrible circumstances develop?
Where did these difficult people come from?
Lord, I need hupomone* today –
The ability to bear up under very difficult experiences,
And not swerve from my faith and sense of purpose.
Please give me makrothumia* as well –
Patience, forbearance, longsuffering,
The ability to put up with difficult people.
Make my life the way You wish, Lord,
But please give me wisdom and patience to endure.
*Greek

God's Word for You
"With all lowliness and meekness, with longsuffering, forbearing one another in love…" Ephesians 4:2

Wealth

Lord, perceiving wealth too dear
Causes disinclination to charity
And tempts to the neglect of justice,
While feeding the habit of selfishness.

It's easy to disregard Your direction, Lord,
And distant myself from others' needs
All for fickle, fleeting finances.
Hoarding wealth has kept many a soul from heaven.

Lord, I will not wallow in perceived wealth.
My wealth lies in generous obedience to Your will.
It's easy to give of my surplus,
Help me give to the point of self-denial.

God's Word for You
*"Give, and it will be given to you. A good measure,
pressed down, shaken together and running over, will
be poured into your lap. For with the measure you use,
it will be measured to you." Luke 6:38*

All

I've experienced
Yearning,
 Waiting,
The edge of despair.
I've known
Dead dreams,
Wasted years,
Endless efforts of futility.
All the past,
Take it, Lord.
I give it with true praise,
Because I know
All I once thought important,
Doesn't truly matter at all.

The future,
The best,
The yet to come,
Might it be,
That it's already here?
My divine dance has begun
With the maker of music,
The Master of song.
I shall twirl, my Lord,
To Your tune now and forever.

God's Word for You
"Praise him with tambourine and dance; praise him with strings and pipe!" Psalm 150:4

Resting in God

Resting in God,
What a desirable position!
Having done all, to stand and wait.
What a rare state, to have truly done all.
Then to completely cease acting,
Surrendering the future to God's will,
While experiencing total security,
And enjoying true serenity.

What a privilege to know this state of being,
To bask in exquisite peace,
Sustained by spiritual energy,
Resting in God.

God's Word for You
"Come to me, all you who are weary and burdened, and I will give you rest. Take my yoke upon you and learn from me, for I am gentle and humble in heart, and you will find rest for your souls." Matthew 11: 28-29

Come & See

Many encouraged me to seek God
With all my being,
They said He would respond,
He even longed for me.

"Come and see who God is.
Linger among His followers"
These people believe God's truly honored
In simple bread and wine.

I said I'll look, I will,
But Christian ways are so strange.
Are these people demented, or am I?
How could they experience the divine?

I needed to know.
Dare I believe?
Should I make this God mine?
Yes, I have! Amen. Hallelujah! It's true!

God's Word for You
*"At that time Jesus, full of joy through the Holy Spirit,
said, 'I praise you, Father, Lord of heaven and earth,
because you have hidden these things from the wise
and learned, and revealed them to little children. Yes,
Father, for this was your good pleasure.'" Luke 10:21*

Heart Guard

It's not an easy thing to guard one's heart.
Within minutes my emotions switch.
Suddenly I'm looking for what I can get,
When I should be a fountain of giving.

Lord, good behavior often stings,
Someone shoots me an unkindness
And my desire to strike back arises with fury.
My heart attitude of peace shatters in seconds.

Lord, I long to have a pure heart,
Guard this heart of mine with holy power.
Help me remember to forego pride and take no
offense.
Let the love that flows through me be Yours.

God's Word for You
*"Above all else, guard your heart, for everything you
do flows from it." Proverbs 4:23*

Communion

Union with a holy God,
How far-fetched can this be?
Immersed in total awareness of Your presence?
I kneel. I wait.
How impossible it seems.
Then
You come,
My words stop,
Meditation deepens,
My being is intensified,
Oh my God,
You're here,
I hold my breath,
I gulp,
Only this,
Only You!

God's Word for You:
"Your law, Spirit of life, has set me free from sin and death." Romans 8:2

Impact

Lord, what an impact You make!
"Lord, Lord," Peter called You and wept,
Paul dropped to the ground,
The healed multitudes praised you,
Pharisaic leaders feared you,
I bow with awe.
I can hardly leave Your presence, Lord,
So sweet is this intimate communion we share.
I must force myself away,
But only for an interval of hours.
While I still live in this flesh, I must rest.
Someday I will be pure spirit, Lord,
And our time together will be limitless ecstasy!

God's Word for You:
"How lovely is your dwelling place,
Lord Almighty!
My soul yearns, even faints,
for the courts of the Lord..."
Psalm 84:1-2

Blackness

Lord, I can't imagine how I would live,
Without knowledge of You at my side,
I close my eyes and try to think
What it would be like to live so all alone.
For its only awareness of You
And access to Your throne,
That fires my mind, and soothes my soul.

Without You I fear blackness would overwhelm me
In the problems, illnesses and general evil of life.
Which sometimes appear greater than my ability to
cope.
When I swirl in emptiness,
God of light, You are my brightness,
You alone dispel all darkness and give me meaning.
I bow before You, humble and grateful,
That we journey through this world together.

God's Word for You
*"The people living in darkness have seen a great light;
on those living in the land of the shadow of death a
light has dawned." Matthew 4:16*

Enemy Territory

Entering temptation is enemy territory.
It's fraught with danger.
I'd never march into evil.
But might I slip in
Or stumble over the edge?

Flirting with wishful thinking is dangerous.
Wallowing in remorse and regret,
Wanting to be like someone else-
The enemy occupies such places.
I need to retreat instantly.

The present moment is where I experience God's
grace.
I shall work with my battalion there,
Following my Divine commander,
Seeking continual discernment,
Staying safe in His embrace.

God's Word for You
*"No temptation has overtaken you except what is
common to mankind. And God is faithful; he will not
let you be tempted beyond what you can bear. But
when you are tempted, he will also provide a way out
so that you can endure it." 1 Corinthians 10:13*

Cleaning

Carpets, windows, walls,
Collect dirt.
So does my life.
Drawers, shelves, counters,
Collect clutter,
So does my life.
Lord, You remind me,
Cleaning is a constant chore
But one with great value.
Polishing has purpose.
It protects and beautifies,
Every area of my home, of my life.
Lord, cleaning my soul can be monotonous,
Help me remember it's part of your plan
To keep me sparkling,
Not just on the outside, but within, too.

God's Word for You
"Then the Lord said to him, 'Now then, you Pharisees clean the outside of the cup and dish, but inside you are full of greed and wickedness. You foolish people! Did not the one who made the outside make the inside also?'"
Luke 11:39 - 40

Offerings

Lord, you detest meaningless offerings.
You warned Your people about this.
What offerings can I make
That would have meaning for You?
I know! A repentant heart of love,
Hands that serve others,
A mind that thinks of You often,
A body that remains holy,
Finances distributed with compassion.
Lord, I want to make such offerings
That will please You in every way.

God's Word for You

"Stop bringing me your meaningless gifts; the incense of your offerings disgusts me! As for your celebrations of the new moon and the Sabbath and your special days for fasting— they are all sinful and false. I want no more of your pious meetings." Isaiah 1:13

Whatever

Goal-setter,
Great dreamer,
Diligent thinker,
List maker extraordinaire,
Yet, often an inadequate doer am I.
Lord, hear my cry,
May my plans find fruition.
Keep my focus on first priorities.
Sharpen my persistence
For Your plans of consequence.

I want to be a whatever person for You, Lord,
Despite my occasional fearful eyes and trembling feet.
With all my heart I say "Yes! Okay."
Have my life Your way,
Wherever You send me, Lord,
Only guide me lest I stray.
Whenever You choose,
I'm willing to move.
Name it, Lord,
I'll be the one,
Empowered by You,
I'm there with You,
Through You, for You,
Whatever!

God's Word for You
"For I know the plans I have for you," declares the LORD, "plans to prosper you and not to harm you, plans to give you hope and a future." Jeremiah 29:11

Great Replacer

Great Replacer
Take from me:
Work without purpose,
Fever of self, cares and fear
Give me activity with meaning,
Love from indifference,
Peace with courage,
Meaning from nothingness,
Joy from despair.

Lord, you will never fail me,
Surely this is true.
How I thirst for faith to believe it more.
Majestic faith huge enough to:
Dash every fear,
Demolish every evil,
Forsake every sin,
Enjoy every blessing.

God's Word for You
"Blessed is the one who does not walk in step with the wicked or stand in the way that sinners take or sit in the company of mockers, but whose delight is in the law of the LORD, and who meditates on his law day and night." Psalm 1: 1-2

The Moments

Give Him the moments
Of your agony,
Incompleteness,
Insignificance,
Of your wishing,
Striving and conniving,
Of Your yearning.
Let Him make the moments
Into a robe of glory.

We can never learn enough,
Buy enough,
Accomplish enough,
Give enough,
Help enough,
To deserve a moment in eternity.
We only need know the One
Who is enough
Who invites us in.

Lord, in love I draw close.
You touch all my moments.
You give comfort when I grieve,
All the wisdom I need.
I depend upon You always,
Holiest of fathers,
Savior and brother Jesus,
Powerful, loving Holy Spirit
Living within me constantly!

Throne Room

Lord, help me keep today in its place
It keeps wanting to slip into tomorrow
Or trying to sneak back to yesterday.
Only this day holds your daily grace.

Lord, I want to stay in the now with You.
And live the way You teach
Moving at a calm and orderly pace
Finding joy immersed in Your grace.

I come before You,
Today again new.
I drop to my knees
Amazed and pleased.

While still in this world
Incomplete and flawed,
I'm taken imaginatively to the throne room
Into Your Presence - My deepest joy.

Different

Distractions,
Attractions
To this and that,
These and those.
My mind flutters
There and here.
Yet I long for You.
I yearn to draw near
Focus my mind and heart,
Teach me how to do my part.

I am more than weak.
I am hopeless and self-absorbed,
I am foolish and silly.
Despite all that I am,
You call me beloved!
Lord You take my weakness
And give me incredible power,
Enormous capability for love,
And great grace to do good.

Lord, I'm still me,
But cleansed and baptized,
I'm the same,
But different too.
My soul is sealed,
My heart is seared,
My spirit is ignited,
My eyes have seen the glory.
I'm me, with You.

Needing Grace

Great grace I would know,
Great good I would do,
Great love I shall give,
Great cost I will pay,
Great God with You!

Lord, I need grace for my spiritual health every day.
I race away from deceivers that murder truth.
I dart from thick walls of doubt that would enclose me.
I scurry from sin that taunts my insecurities
I flee fires of resentment that destroy love.
I dash from floods of fear that would drown me.
I zoom from Satan's wily tricks.
Lord, watch me move,
I'm on the grace run to win.
One day I'll shout with triumph
As I give my torch to the next generation.

Papa

I'm grateful to You, Papa,
For life, work, hope,
Stones, wishes,
Crosses, bridges,
Success, laughter,
Failure, trust,
 Tears, power,
For now, for what's next,
For time and limits,
And all that has been
In me and about me
On earth and in heaven.

Papa, you are to me:
Mighty master,
Great grace-giver,
Awesome life-builder,
Fantastic future-maker!
I can't see the way each day, but
Lord, in You I trust.
You bring order to chaos,
Plenty for lack, strength for fear
How gracious Your kindness is,
I receive Your help with humility,
And bow before You in honor.

Fear

Spirit of fear, there you are again.
Wanting to suck up my peace.
Tricking me with your taunts.
Biting me your what-ifs.
Troubling my sleep.
Away with you.
I'm God's child,
He has set me free.
And wants me to live free.
I'm shutting my mind to you.
Back to hell you go!

The Jesus Life

Walking,
Wanting,
Waiting.

Praying,
Praising,
Pressing On.

Loving,
Laughing,
Listening.

Seeped in Jesus
Washed with joy!
This is the Jesus life!

Glory-found,
Glory-bound
Glory-crowned.

Glory! What a word,
What an idea,
What a reality!

I asked to see,
You let me glimpse,
Not with my eyes but my heart.
Denial fled, it's true,
Your Glory permeates the universe.
Glorious Jesus, You fill me with awe!

One Night

Angels guard me close.
Amazing as it is,
Your master calls me His,
And finds me precious.
One night
With God,
Real,
Intimate,
Soul- stretching,
Body-blasting.
One night and
Life forever
Can never be the same.

Love

Lord, You love me!
I will scream it,
Shout it,
Dance about it.
God that you would –
That you could -
Or ever should –
Love me!
And not just me,
But the entire world!
Lord I desire to be connected,
Ever entangled and tight,
Never torn loose.
Make me thrive,
Only in you can I survive
Lord, you give my soul its glow
And take me deep into joy
What a thrill to know I belong,
To the one who's loved me all along.
The Lord of joy,
Lord of laughs,
Lord of roars
What wondrous fun
In the presence of the Holy One!

God's Word for You
"How priceless is your unfailing love, O God! People take refuge in the shadow of your wings." Psalm 36:7

Our World

Lord,
Do you ever get weary
Watching our world,
Crazed beyond control,
Twisting and turning,
Churning with hate,
Raging with war,
Seething with self?
Thoughts are formed without facts.
Men hate without cause.
People die without love.
Children live without protection.
Many in our world
Refuse with final breaths
To accept you Jesus,
You, Who alone brings sense,
You Who teaches love,
Personifies truth.
Awesome Jesus,
Who will come again
Flood this world with love,
To forever end hate,
And transform this chaotic world.

God's Word for You
"The Lord our God is merciful and forgiving, even though we have rebelled against him; we have not obeyed the Lord our God or kept the laws he gave us through his servants the prophets." Daniel 9:9-10

Responsibility

Master, I accept Your command.
I desire Your will.
My aim is the Kingdom.
I'm alert and ready.
Thank you, Lord, for wisdom to set my pace,
Propel me, Lord, constrain me,
Until Your perfect will accomplished.
I'll take any action You wish,
I'll act or wait.
As long as necessary.
The hour to enter my Kingdom life I don't know,
The Maker of Time I do know.

God's Word for You
"Therefore, my beloved brothers, be steadfast, immovable, always abounding in the work of the Lord, knowing that in the Lord your labor is not in vain." 1 Corinthians 15:58

Attack

The clouds are chasing me today.
Darkness, fear, condemnation.
I run from beneath.
But they're gaining Lord.
Those nasty should-haves,
The wily if-onlys,
And wearisome watch-outs
Are floating about everywhere.

Lord, ugly worries are on the prowl
Attacking me again.
Telling me to fret and fear.
I laugh to myself.
I'm on to them now,
I know their plan -
To suck away my joy,
And rob me of peace.

Today they'll fail.
I've shored up my strength,
I smile and rejoice,
No way will I succumb,
I'll give them no place,
Here in the place of the sun
Where Your brightness covers me.
Into your arms holy One,
Come the worries, Lord, cast away.

"Be sober, be vigilant; because your adversary the devil, as a roaring lion, walks about, seeking whom he may devour: resist steadfast in the faith." 1Peter 8-9

Astonishment

Jesus, You astonished the Nazarenes in the synagogue
With Word of Your mighty works and power
And amazing wisdom acquired without learning.
They scoffed, disapproved, refused to believe.
No god from among the Nazarenes could come!
Their lack of faith displeased You.
Doubt blocked Your power.
Your miracles were limited to healing just a few,
And quickly You withdrew.
Lord, may I astonish You
With unfailing, outrageous belief.

God's Word for You
"Truly I tell you," He [Jesus] continued, "no prophet is accepted in his hometown." Luke 4:24

At The Well

How I love to ponder this request:
Meet me at the well today, Lord,
I need to visualize your face.
I long to hear your voice.
My soul is thirsty, Lord.
I'm bringing my water jug
For a refill of living water
That only You can give.

The commitments of today are calling.
Great and gracious Jesus,
Incomparable Holy Spirit,
Majestic, magnificent Father,
Come with me,
Through this day.
Infuse my words and actions
With your Divine Presence.

Lord, as I meditate on You,
You take me to places and feelings
Warm and wonderful.
The demands of today fade away.
I'm totally at peace.
I need nothing,
You are everything.
You are my confidence, my all.

"Whoever dwells in the shelter of the Most High will rest in the shadow of the Almighty. I will say of the Lord, "He is my refuge and my fortress, my God, in whom I trust." Psalm 91:1-2

Touching God

Jesus, I'm amazed!
In Mark's Gospel record of your deeds
While You walked among us,
Friends brought their sick to You
That they might touch Your garment
And those who touched You were healed.
Lord, I thought You had to touch them,
But it was in their reaching for You
That the miracle happened.
Lord, I need a miracle.
I'm reaching.

God's Word for You
"And wherever he went—into villages, towns or countryside—they placed the sick in the marketplaces. They begged him to let them touch even the edge of his cloak, and all who touched it were healed." Mark 6:56

Breathless

Lord, I often hold my breath
When thinking of You,
Because breathing might disturb
My overwhelming awareness of You.

If others perceive me strange,
As perhaps they shall,
Since such faith is foreign to current culture.
I will only sigh and say, "Their loss."

If only they knew You, Lord,
They would understand the passion.
That enables me to love without hesitation,
Free from doubt.

I live with proven faith,
And a steadfast spirit,
Approved for the kingdom crown.
Because of You, Lord, this is me.

God's Word for You
"I will sing of the Lord's great love forever; with my mouth I will make your faithfulness known through all generations. I will declare that your love stands firm forever, that you have established your faithfulness in heaven itself." Psalm 89: 11-2

Mary's Faith

Mary, what would have happened
Had you not believed what the angel Gabriel said?
Would another have been chosen?
Had you refused could another woman have been found
With Your level of holiness?
Mary, such speculation is foolish,
God knew the depth of your faith
Even though you asked, "How can this be, I'm a virgin?"
You questioned only the process,
But there was never a doubt,
You'd do what God asked.
You believed in the One who commanded these events
And knew He could bring them to pass.
Did you waver?
Not a bit!
Nor may I,
Whatever God asks of me!

God's Word for You
"The angel went to her and said, "Greetings, you who are highly favored! The Lord is with you." Luke 1:28

Pick and Choose

Not all Your words, Lord!
I'd much prefer to choose.

If it's all the same to You.
 I'd like to skip
Fasting,
Penitence,
Humility,
Affliction and
Sacrifice.

Don't get me wrong.
I like Your other words:
Love,
Peace,
Joy,
Blessing, and
Anointing.

But Lord, I know I can't pick and choose,
So help me please.
May I accept and embrace all
That living
For You,
With You,
And in You means.

"For the grace of God has appeared that offers salvation to all people. It teaches us to say 'No' to ungodliness and worldly passions, and to live self-controlled, upright and godly lives in this present age."
Titus 2:11-12

Pride

Pride popped up.
It surprised me.
I sighed and pushed it away.
I thought I was long ago free.
Pop-push, it's back,
 Push-pop temptation.
Lord, I need to know,
Will all my life be like this?
"Yes," Lord, You say,
"Until in My presence
With total humility
You forever stay."

God's Word for You
"For all have sinned and fall short of the glory of God, and all are justified freely by his grace through the redemption that came by Christ Jesus."
Romans 3:23-24

Daily Joys

Lord, I'm finding joy everywhere.
In oatmeal and hot tea,
The first brush of morning air upon my face.
The car that takes me farther than I can walk.
The phone that connects me to those I love
Who aren't with me.

I'm savoring joy in simple moments,
In preparing food and making choices,
Raising the blinds,
In the touch of love -
A pat, a kiss or hug.
In work I know I can complete.

Joy is everywhere.
Why should I indulge in worry
Or trouble my soul with care?
Lord, I'm filled with awe.
 I thank you.
I am so blessed.

Lord, I purpose in my heart today
To accomplish what most pleases You.
To follow Your teaching and guidance,
Holding my heart close to Yours.
Help me, Lord, I pray.
To make the most of this day.

"But blessed are your eyes, because they see; and your ears, because they hear. I tell you the truth, many prophets and righteous people longed to see what you see, but they didn't see it. And they longed to hear what you hear, but they didn't hear it."
Matthew 13:16-17

Angel Joy

More joy in heaven?
How can heaven's happiness possibly be increased?
Yet one wicked person repents, turns,
Has a twist of mind,
Sees "sin" as sin,
Abhors deeds that lead to spiritual death,
And Your Word says the angels rejoice.
Incredible!
I've created joy in heaven.
Angels have rejoiced over me -
I'm an angel joy-giver!

God's Word for You
"In the same way, I tell you, there is joy in the presence of the angels of God over one sinner who repents." Luke 15:10

Focus

When all of me is
Focused on all of You
I fade in my own significance.
I experience the me you intend I be.

You fill me with a driving desire to
Honor and glorify You.
Finally, truly, amazingly,
I know You as my healer and protector

Body-healer,
Mind-healer,
Heart-healer.
Heal me God!

Body-protector,
Mind-protector,
Life is often hard.
Protect me God!

The world would tempt me away.
Guard me God,
Keep me safe.
Never let me stray.

Lord, I find my delight in You -
Beyond words,
Beyond comprehension,
Beyond my wildest imagination.

Hurry-Scurry

The hurry-scurry of my life exhausts me
I often choose to do too much.
Then struggle to perform
All that I said I would.

I dread to disappoint others,
But will overextend myself,
Rushing at an unnatural pace.
Lord, where is my still space?
.
Help me choose more wisely
Keep me from performance worry
And stop my hurry-scurry.
May only Your perfect plan guide me.

Death

Death would steal my life.
Lord You bid it wait.
Its fear power is great
In people unsure of their fate.

Lord, thanks to You,
Death is to me but
A leap over the wall,
An opening of the garden gate.

Now here, then there,
With man, with God.
A sunset on earth,
A sunrise in heaven.

I must remember,
I've nothing to fear.
Death does not steal my life.
It transports me to its fullness.

God's Word for You

"But, in fact, Christ has been raised from the dead, the first fruits of those who have fallen asleep. For as by a man came death, by a man has come also the resurrection of the dead. For as in Adam all die, so also in Christ shall all be made alive."
1 Corinthians 15:20-21

Sorry

Lord,
Rumors spread everywhere.
What did it feel like
To be talked about by many?
I'd hate it Lord.
Did it bother You?
I mean I know you withdrew,
But didn't it hurt very deep?
Even though Your rejection wasn't new.

Honored one moment
Then
Feared,
Hated,
Pushed
And driven away.

Do You hear repentance now?
"Sorry."
That simple, humble word of strength?
Spoken by hearts who know,
Heavy with the weight of wrongs.
I hope so.
Hear it from me:
"Sorry."

"Then I acknowledged my sin to You and did not cover up my iniquity. I said, 'I will confess my transgressions to the Lord.' And You forgave the guilt of my sin." Psalm 32:5

One Thousand

Lord, looking back I can recall
More than one thousand thoughts of You.
One thousand rainy days with sunshine.
One thousand experiences of pleasure,
One thousand smiles within my soul.
Precious protections placed,
Desperate needs met,
Frantic prayers answered,
Amazing love,
Restoring grace.
I bow, amazed to be so blessed.
Your presence is exquisite!
I urge others to try the Lord.
You'll see,
God will do for you,
What He did for me.
And turn every humdrum day
Into a masterpiece.

God's Word for You
"God is faithful for all He has promised."
Hebrews 11:23

Glistening

Lord, how I long to have been there,
When You traveled a mountain's distance away from
the ordinary.
To show Peter, James and John.
Your glistening garment
Your resplendent divinity.
Joined by Elijah, and Moses via clouds.
And the Words of Your Father.
What did His voice sound like?
A river flowing,
Thunder breaking,
Silk rustling?
His Words were
Simple, clear,
"Listen and obey my Son."
Lord, I long to see the glistening garment
And hear the sound of God.
Lord, my heart shouts
"I love you, I will obey.
Only take me to You someday."

God's Word for You
*"After six days Jesus took with him Peter, James and
John the brother of James, and led them up a high
mountain by themselves. There he was transfigured
before them. His face shone like the sun, and his
clothes became as white as the light." Matthew 17:1-2*

Envisioning

My Healer, my Joy,
I dance before You,
Envisioning Your throne.
You bid me come close.
Praise streams from my soul.
My surroundings become like mist.
Oh what You've done for me!
I can hardly take it in.
Nothing seems real,
Except You alone.

What was it like Lord,
Making that flight to heaven from earth?
What's it like at the right hand of God?
How can You be near me and there, too?
What will my mansion be like?
I can't imagine
 The length of forever,
The beauty of perfection,
Your face, my King.

God's Word for You
"Eye has not seen, *nor ear heard, Nor have entered into the heart of man The things which God has prepared for those who love Him." 1 Corinthians 2:9*

Gehenna

Gehenna, even the word sounds abhorrent.
Supreme sight of misery.
Worms that cannot die preying endlessly,
Salting with fire that's continuous.
Such agony I can't comprehend.
What horror we inflict on ourselves by our sins!
Lord, have mercy!
May every sinner repent
Before it's too late.
Even the word sin sounds ugly.
Sin spells bondage extraordinary.
I alone decide:
Yukky, sticky, messy life or
Gorgeous, bright life.
Obedience brings freedom forever,
Goodness unparalleled,
Joy beyond definition.
The decision is easy.

God's Word for You
"Then He will also say to those on His left, 'Depart from Me, accursed ones, into the eternal fire which has been prepared for the devil and his angels."
Matthew 25:41

Twelve Years

Lord, You knew Your power had gone forth
You stopped the crowd
And demanded to know who touched You.
"Yes, it's me," the woman said.
"I touched your garment, I did it to be healed."

"Your confidence in Me is great," You said.
"It has caused your healing."
Lord, what 12 years of physicians' efforts
Couldn't produce
Occurred in one touch of You.

"Trust has made you well," You said.
"Now enjoy peace and wellness."
Lord, You were impressed,
At the faith her action professed.
Make my faith strong, as well, Lord.

I need to touch You, Master.
Life makes me bleed
And the flow doesn't stop
Heal my mind, body and soul.
Only You can make me whole.

God's Word for You
"When she heard about Jesus, she came up behind him in the crowd and touched his cloak, because she thought, 'If I just touch his clothes, I will be healed.'

Immediately her bleeding stopped and she felt in her body that she was freed from her suffering."
Mark 5: 27-28

Skyward

Eagles soar, but shall I?
Yes, Lord, You say,
 Catch flight with the Divine Spirit
Who creates holiness and happiness.
Why, precious child, would you settle for less?
Come Spirit, swoop me up!
I want to fly.
Keep my flight balanced
Between gazing up and looking out.
Let me remember often to glance skyward
Lest this life absorb too much focus,
With its pull of material toys
And lure of impermanent joys.
May I be a busy, earthly Christian
As well as a consistent cloud-watcher.
Spirit-soaring skyward while waiting for your return.

God's Word for You
"But because of his great love for us, God, who is rich in mercy, made us alive with Christ. It is by grace you have been saved." Ephesians 2:4-5

Scorn

Jairus' girl is dead, bystanders said,
As they jeered and made fun of You, Lord,
They laughed with scorn
And ignored Your power,
As they proceeded to mourn.

"Simply believe and she'll be well," You said.
You grasped her hand.
"Back from death," You made the demand.
And upon Your command,
The precious child's spirit returned.

Having beheld Your light.
To the amazement of all,
The girl arose with the glow of life,
Her parents, no longer bereft,
Exchanged their tears for delight.

How I wish I'd been there.
I've always wondered,
What did the scorners say then
When the weeping and wailing was quelled.
When what they'd thought impossible became true?

Lord, over and over You reveal Yourself,
But those too full of themselves
With minds of stone,
Refuse to believe Who You are,
And the miracles You can do.

Lord, if there's any trace within Me
Of cynicism or doubt, I pray, root it out.
Fill me with Your light and truth
That I too may speak forth miracles
With the power Your Spirit provides.

God's Word for You

"They started making fun of [Jesus], so he put them all out, took the child's father and mother and his three disciples, and went into the room where the child was lying. He took her by the hand and said to her, 'Talitha, koum,' which means, 'Little girl, I tell you to get up!' She got up at once and started walking around. (She was twelve years old.) When this happened, they were completely amazed."
Mark 5:40-42

The Agenda

Good morning Jesus.
I visualize You sitting at my kitchen table.
"What's the agenda for today?" I ask.
You reply,
"I have your schedule ready, I always do."
Have no concern,
Go and do, listen as I guide.

And, oh, along the way
Two special things to remember.
The enemy would give you worry about your health.
I'll handle that.
He'd also like you to have concern about time or
money.
Fearful about having enough.
I'll manage that.

You've been timid in these areas, your enemy's
observed.
Use the positive authority I've given you.
Speak My Word into all situations.
Work My plan,
Then trust me, I'll do the rest.
Have no concern,
Know always My way is best."

99 Trustworthy

99 sheep left alone in the wilderness,
While the search for the lost one proceeded.
99 Sheep who could be trusted to stay alone.
The shepherd knew their strengths and their limits.
What confidence the Shepherd had
To depend on the faithfulness of 99.
Who would not venture from God's boundaries.
Lord I wish to be as reliable.
Give me staying power
That You may always depend upon me.

God's Word for You
"Suppose one of you has a hundred sheep and loses one of them. Doesn't he leave the ninety-nine in the open country and go after the lost sheep until he finds it?" Luke 15:4

Words

Lord, precise words matter to You.
You know they reveal the heart.
A Greek woman begged,
She needed a demon to leave her girl.
You initially said you wouldn't help,
"Jews came first."
She asked only for Your healing crumbs.
You heard faith in her words.
Because of that You released the power to heal.
You told her, "Your daughter's demon has fled."
Lord, may my heart,
My thoughts, my words,
My total being,
Also be filled with belief
I long to honor You with my faith,
And release Your power in the world.

God's Word for You
"Then she came and worshiped Him, saying, 'Lord, help me!' But He answered and said, 'It is not good to take the children's bread and throw it to the little dogs.' And she said, 'Yes, Lord, yet even the little dogs eat the crumbs which fall from their masters' table.' Then Jesus answered and said to her, 'O woman, great is your faith! Let it be to you as you desire.' And her daughter was healed from that very hour."
Matthew 15: 25-28

Divine

Divine Ear,
Hear me.
Divine Eye,
See me.
Divine Hand,
Guide me.
Divine heart,
Hold me.
Divine Lord,
Protect me,
I am Yours.
Astounded

I marvel, Lord,
At Your
Might,
Magnificence,
And
Majesty.
You astound me.
How I applaud You,
My great God!

God's Word for You

"I pray to you, O God, because you answer me; so turn to me and listen to my words. Reveal your wonderful love and save me; at your side I am safe from my enemies." Psalm 17:6-7

Squeeze

Possessions

Possessions pull and demand,
Clamor for more comes from my soul
And never seems to end:
Seek more, not less.
This quest entices and entraps me.
Why do I cling to and demand
That which steals my contentment,
And robs me of a peaceful life?
I must seek less, not more,
Not be a fool.
Enough my soul!
Lord, You say
It's not a simple move
Getting through that narrow door
You say, "Strive to enter."
And You give Your assurance,
Entrance is possible.
Yet, many will be turned away,
Considered unknown,
Even though they speak Your name.

God's Word for You
*"Enter through the narrow gate. For wide is the gate
and broad is the road that leads to destruction, and
many enter through it. But small is the gate and narrow
the road that leads to life, and only a few find it."*
Matthew 7:13-14

Blood

The blood I draw from others is not red,
Like the blood drawn from Abel or Zechariah.
It is invisible.
But I too steal lifeblood
When I kill someone's joy with my tongue,
 When I steal human dignity with my thoughts,
When I destroy another's peace by my behavior.
Help me be a lifeblood-giver, not taker.
Your blood, My Lord, was enough sacrifice
To last through eternity.

God's Word for You
"And the word of the Lord came again to Zechariah: 'This is what the Lord Almighty said: 'Administer true justice; show mercy and compassion to one another. Do not oppress the widow or the fatherless, the foreigner or the poor. Do not plot evil against each other.'"
Zechariah 7:8-10

Topsy-Turvy God

Topsy-turvy God,
You tell me little is big,
Great is small,
Emptiness (of self)
Is fullness (of You).
In weakness is strength.
Waiting is doing.
Helping is praying.
Proud before others,
Detestable before God.
Without worldly value,
Of great importance to You.
If you say how a thing is,
My topsy-turvy God,
I know Your words are true.
Topsy-turvy God,
Keep me right side up.

God's Word for You
"My mouth will tell of your righteous deeds, of your saving acts all day long, though I know not how to relate them all." Psalm 71:15

Impulsive

Lord,
You loved
Impulsive
Peter.

Even though
He was
Most assuredly,
Often a pest.

Rushing,
Eager to do,
Anything he could
For You.

Me, too, Lord
Forgive me
When
I've hurried ahead.

What's the plan
For today?
I'm ready
To be led.

God's Word for You

"Jesus turned and said to Peter, 'Get behind me, Satan! You are a stumbling block to me; you do not have in mind the concerns of God, but merely human concerns.'" Matthew 16:23

Spirit Sounds

Sounds of the Spirit among us:
A poor person eats,
A pastor counsels,
A friend listens,
A child receives instruction,
A son is rebuked,
A lonely woman knows comfort,
A depressed person opens a door,
A sick person prays for healing,
A grieving spouse laughs again.

*"And I will ask the Father, and he will give you
another advocate to help you and be with you
forever." John 14:16*

Gardener

Lord, My Gardener
Sprinkle Your seed, stabilize my roots.
Water me well that I may grow strong.

My outer life,
My inner life.
Lord, make them match.

I don't want to be a secret-keeper
Hiding part of who I am.
Dishonesty doesn't honor You.

Let all of me
Always be worthy for all to see,
May I blossom well for thee.

I long to hear and heed Your truth
On Your Word I'll feed daily.
And depend on You for my every need.

God's Word for You
"As for what was sown on good soil, this is the one who hears the word and understands it. He indeed bears fruit and yields, in one case a hundredfold, in another sixty, and in another thirty." Luke 13:23

Works and Soap

Lord, I need to ask You,
Just as Your disciples asked,
I really must know,
What am I to do
That I may be working the works of God?

Lord, I sense Your reply.
The work You ask of me
Is believing in You, trusting and relying on You.
Lord, it sounds too simple,
Why do I often make it hard?

And Lord You have different thoughts
About cleanliness!
Can You clarify them please?
Outside clean, inside dirty?
Outside dirty, inside clean?

You say,
What comes out is unclean,
What goes in can cleanse.
Lord, You alone can remove all that defiles.
Wash me well, Lord, and often
Keep me hallowed and clean.

God's Word for You
"Again Jesus called the crowd to him and said, 'Listen to me, everyone, and understand this. Nothing outside a person can defile them by going into them. Rather, it is what comes out of a person that defiles them.'"
Mark 7:14-16.

Jesus' Hands

Jesus, I'm pondering Your hands,
Comfortable handling carpenter's tools,
Callused from laboring as a woodworker,
Familiar with ordinary beds, tables, chests.
Jesus, You impacted manual effort with honor,
Treading on sawdust and shavings,
Soon to create not with wood and nails
But with eternal love and truth.
Jesus, Your hands pierced wood with nails,
Then themselves were pierced by nails.
Wood-working Son of God,
Now You work on human spirits,
Crafting them for divine use.

God's Word for You
"And he went throughout all Galilee, teaching in their synagogues and proclaiming the gospel of the kingdom and healing every disease and every affliction among the people." Matthew 4:23

Refreshment

Off to the hills you went
You took Your leave, Lord
From the throngs of people
Sending even Your beloved disciples away.
You sought to be alone.

But not completely by Yourself.
You desired, needed, to be
In the Presence of The Father.
He alone could provide the refreshment
You required so sorely.

The Father fed you well.
Daily restored and renewed,
You were able to take up
Your intense quest for lost hearts
And resume your earth journey.

Lord, I'm off to the hills of my heart
For my refreshment.
Father, Son and Spirit,
I have total confidence that You
Will meet me there.

God's Word for You
"Then Jesus ordered him, 'Don't tell anyone, but go, show yourself to the priest and offer the sacrifices that Moses commanded for your cleansing.' Crowds of people came to hear Jesus and to be healed of their sicknesses. But Jesus often withdrew to lonely places and prayed." Luke 5:14-15

248

Pressure

My internal alarm sounds.
The pressure I don't want
Sneaks upon me.

My head pounds
And tension tightens.
Stress speaks the devil's words:

Do more, do it quicker,
Strive without ceasing
Or your needs will never be met.

But Lord,
I know this isn't Your way.
Why do I fall into this trap?

You want me stress-free,
You meet my every need
When I calmly follow Your lead.
You allow me to reap
Where I haven't even sown.
And give me benefits undeserved.

Help me push stress away.
And let it not control me today.
I will trust my Lord of Peace.

Why should I strive endlessly,
When it's Your hand that gives blessing?
You desire that I maintain my peace.

God's Word for You
"I denied myself nothing my eyes desired; I refused my heart no pleasure. My heart took delight in all my labor, and this was the reward for all my toil. Yet when I surveyed all that my hands had done and what I had toiled to achieve, everything was meaningless, a chasing after the wind; nothing was gained under the sun.
Ecclesiastes 2:10-11

Thank You

Thank you is an important thing to say
And an ideal way to start each day
How grateful I am to you, Lord,
For keeping my loved ones safe
And daily transforming us,
Making us more like You.
I forsake all fear
And raise my shield of faith.
I thrust my sword of truth,
My King will always give me victory.
Thank You my Lord and my God.

God's Word for You
"Let the message of Christ dwell among you richly as you teach and admonish one another with all wisdom through psalms, hymns, and songs from the Spirit, singing to God with gratitude in your hearts."
Colossians 3:16

Seeker

Sinners, come, draw near.
Shocking as it would seem,
This Man Who is God
Welcomes you to dine,
He receives you in your sinful state
Showing He loves the reprobate.

If you choose to let Him
He'll change you inside
A cleansing He'll create.
He'll welcome you
As he welcomed me.
Come, draw near.

God's Word for You
"That which was from the beginning, which we have heard, which we have seen with our eyes, which we have looked at and our hands have touched— The life appeared; we have seen it and testify to it, and we proclaim to you the eternal life, which was with the Father and has appeared to us." 1 John 1-2

Fig Tree

Fig tree, fig tree,
Where is your fruit?
Greenery without fruit is unacceptable.
Showy, aren't you?
Lush with potential,
But soon to die.

Doomed to wither you will be.
For barrenness without cause.
Death is your reward,
Your nature was to flourish,
Yet you stand visible to all,
Without fulfilling your purpose.

Lord, I wish to be a great fruit-bearer.
May my branches flourish with lushness.

God's Word for You

"Seeing in the distance a fig tree in leaf, He went to find out if it had any fruit. When he reached it, he found nothing but leaves, because it was not the season for figs. Then he said to the tree, 'May no one ever eat fruit from you again.'" Mark 11:13-14

Enough

Lord, before I knew You,
I feared not being good enough.
Never being worthy,
To merit an eternity of heavenly joy.
How excited I was to learn
I didn't have to be anything.
Your conquest at Calvary,
Was enough for me.

But since, then Lord,
I've feared not doing enough
To prove worthy of Your great love.
How many souls can I help save for You?
How many lives can I help make right?

Enough, You say, cease!
I give freedom, not frenzy.
Don't exchange one bondage for another.

It's not by your doing that You most please Me,
But by time You spend alone with Me.
Lord, I come.

God's Word for You
"Such confidence we have through Christ before God.
Not that we are competent in ourselves to claim
anything for ourselves, but our competence comes
from God. He has made us competent as ministers of a
new covenant..." 2 Corinthians 3:4-6

Mistakes Redeemed

Zachary, lack of faith got you in trouble,
Stripped you of the power of speech for a time.
Lord, feed my faith,
Lest it waver.

Peter, three times You denied Jesus,
Three times I will proclaim,
You alone are holy, holy, holy!
My awesome Lord!

I have sinned against Your commands,
Sadly, countless times, by omission and commission,
Yet always You've loved and forgiven me,
Amazing! Jesus, I will bless Your name forever.

God's Word for You
"I will extol You, my God, O King;
And I will bless Your name forever and ever."
Psalm 145:1

Rejection

As you know well, Lord, I've been rejected,
Felt extreme emotional hurt and pain,
Experienced its excruciating shame,
Even as I tried not to let it show.

Lord, rejection hurts horribly.
That's why it means so much to know,
With unending gratitude
That I need never feel unloved or alone.

You will not reject me.
Emotional security is unfamiliar to me,
But more welcome than I can say.
I gratefully bow in adoration.

God's Word for You
"What then shall we say to these things?
If God is for us, who can be against us?"
Romans 8:31

Jesus, My King

Jesus, You are My King.
I am but a faithful subject.
You direct my deeds.
I serve with confidence,
Gratefully I enter Your presence,
Joyfully, I fulfill Your commands.
You elicit my eternal loyalty,
What sweet service is mine,
What guarantee of reward divine.

Sweet King Jesus,
Dispenser of Mercy,
Giver of Favor,
Reliever of Affliction,
Fortress of Strength,
Beacon of Wisdom,
Refuge of my soul,
What a blessing to serve You.

How precious You are to me.
You're my model for behavior.
Like You, I shall be relaxed and confident,
Bold with assurance,
Soaked in the love of the Father,
Secured by the indwelling Holy Spirit,
Speaking truth clearly and emphatically,
To elicit compelling responses.

"Looking unto Jesus the author and finisher of our faith; who for the joy that was set before him endured the cross, despising the shame, and is set down at the right hand of the throne of God." Hebrews 12:2

A Moment

Is anything more special than a moment?
A dot of time filled with possibilities.
Love to be spent,
Actions to be done,
Skirmishes to be won,
Ideas to be explored.
Forever is but such moments
Strung together as precious pearls -
The essence of God's Kingdom begun
On the filament of now.

God's Word for You
"For God says, "At just the right time, I heard you. On the day of salvation, I helped you." Indeed, the "right time" is now. Today is the day of salvation."
2 Corinthians 6:2

The Gift of Intellect

The real that is unseen,
Is more real than that which is seen.
Sustaining Power, unobservable, untouchable,
Permeates each present moment
And fuses the past with the future.
The supreme source of every atom,
Without effective equal or opposition,
Is Christ, the reality undergirding all.

Living in the world requires exposure to its intellectual
culture,
Being not of the world means not being mastered by it.
Lord, you call us to use the gift of intellect well.
You always encourage evaluation and thinking,
The mind is to be stretched, constantly expanding.
The brain is to be a fact collector and checker,
Feasting on knowledge, digested with wisdom,
May I use my intellect superbly for Your glory.

God's Word for You
*"Blessed is the one who finds wisdom, and the one
who gets understanding, for the gain from her is better
than gain from silver and her profit better than gold."*
Proverbs 3:13

Every Detail

Lord, Your way is best.
Living with every detail
Consecrated to You:
Every word,
Every dream,
Every deed
Every pain
Every joy.
Loving much, loving well.

Lord, as I still my mind,
And gaze upon Your creation,
Joy slips over my soul,
Followed by a lovely flood of Spirit sensation.
My physical body seems to disappear,
I sense only You.

God's Word for You
"But as for me, the nearness of God is my good; I have made the Lord God my refuge, that I may tell of all Your works." Psalm 73:28

Trudging

Lord, I don't like being filled with turmoil,
Lugging through my commitments.
My responsibilities feel too heavy
 For my personal power.
I need some Spirit-nudging.
Prioritize, sift and sort my work.
Remind me of my primary purpose again.

Return to me the essence of joy
During this time of drudgery.
Lord, only by Your authority,
Only in Your presence,
Through Your power,
All that is unfolding
Through Your gracious Hand will be good.

God's Word for You
"And we know that all things work together for good to them that love God, to them who are the called according to his purpose." Romans 8:28

Enigma

Lord, my love for You is intense and fierce
It amazes and energizes me.
Lord, I feel independent and most fully myself
When I'm totally dependent on Your Holy Spirit.
Life with You is exciting, mysterious, and complete.

Lord, you won't hear me asking this question,
"Who will be greatest in the kingdom of heaven?"
I'm content to be the lowest
Just to enter is enough.
All I want is to be included,
And not excluded, forever.

After a glimpse of Your glory.
Lord, I'll be speechless and overwhelmed,
You'll find me flat on my face,
Totally prostrate before You,
Just to be there with You, Lord,
Is all I will ever need.

You'll hear no wishing
For a higher place from me.
To be in Your presence,
Experiencing the fullness of Your majesty,
Is quite enough thrill,
To last throughout every moment of eternity.

"At that time the disciples came to Jesus and asked, 'Who, then, is the greatest in the kingdom of heaven?' He called a little child to him, and placed the child among them. And Jesus said: 'Truly I tell you, unless you change and become like little children, you will never enter the kingdom of heaven. Therefore, whoever takes the lowly position of this child is the greatest in the kingdom of heaven." Matthew 18:1-4

Layers of Life

Lord, I finally understand.
Life is about layers
Like paint layered on a canvas.
The picture starts with rough brush strokes,
Then is defined with more precision,
Adding layers of depth and meaning
Until fine art is produced,
A work of genuine quality - an excellent life.
At times I'm tempted to stop too soon,
Thinking the work is done,
When more touches are needed.
Patience and perseverance are required,
To make my life into a masterpiece for You.

God's Word for You
"You make known to me the path of life; You will fill me with joy in your presence, with eternal pleasures at your right hand." Psalm 16:11

ACKNOWLEDGEMENTS

Thanks to my mom, Bernice Vandy, for leading me to my first experience with memorizing Scripture. My father, Chester Vandy, saw to it that my siblings Jim, Joy and I were brought up with an awareness of God. I'm forever grateful for this foundation. Last, but most significant of all, I appreciate my husband, Wayne, my partner on this exciting life journey.

ABOUT THE AUTHOR

Dr. Judith Rolfs, author, speaker and Christian marriage and family counselor for over twenty-five years, delights in spending time with God the Father, Son and Holy Spirit.

Her books have been distributed worldwide to help others connect intimately with God and enjoy a happy, fulfilling marriage and family life.

Visit her website
www.judithrolfs.com

View her blog at
www.judithrolfs.blogspot.com

Her amazon author page is:
amazon.com/Judith-Rolfs/e/B001KI0KLU

Subscribe to her YouTube channel "Judith Rolfs" for marriage, parenting and life enrichment videos.